NEW DIRECTIONS FOR INSTITUTIONAL RESEARCH

J. Fredericks Volkwein, *Penn State University*
EDITOR-IN-CHIEF

Balancing Qualitative and Quantitative Information for Effective Decision Support

Richard D. Howard
Montana State University–Bozeman

Kenneth W. Borland Jr.
East Stroudsburg University

EDITORS

Number 112, Winter 2001

JOSSEY-BASS
A Wiley Company
www.josseybass.com

BALANCING QUALITATIVE AND QUANTITATIVE INFORMATION FOR EFFEC-
TIVE DECISION SUPPORT
Richard D. Howard, Kenneth W. Borland Jr. (eds.)
New Directions for Institutional Research, no. 112
J. Fredericks Volkwein, Editor-in-Chief

New Directions for Institutional Research is indexed in *College Student
Personnel Abstracts, Contents Pages in Education,* and *Current Index to Journals in Education* (ERIC).

Microfilm copies of issues and chapters are available in 16mm and 35mm,
as well as microfiche in 105mm, through University Microfilms Inc., 300
North Zeeb Road, Ann Arbor, Michigan 48106–1346.

ISSN 0271-0579   electronic ISSN 1536-075X   ISBN 0-7879-5796-8

NEW DIRECTIONS FOR INSTITUTIONAL RESEARCH is part of The Jossey-Bass
Higher and Adult Education Series and is published quarterly by Jossey-
Bass, 989 Market Street, San Francisco, California 94103-1741 (publica-
tion number USPS 098-830). Periodicals postage paid at San Francisco,
California, and at additional mailing offices. POSTMASTER: Send address
changes to New Directions for Institutional Research, Jossey-Bass, 989
Market Street, San Francisco, California 94103-1741.

SUBSCRIPTIONS cost $65 for individuals and $125 for institutions, agencies, and libraries.

EDITORIAL CORRESPONDENCE should be sent to J. Fredericks Volkwein,
Center for the Study of Higher Education, Penn State University, 400
Rackley Building, University Park, PA 16801-5252.

Photograph of the library by Michael Graves at San Juan Capistrano by
Chad Slattery © 1984. All rights reserved.

www.josseybass.com

Printed in the United States of America on acid-free recycled paper con-
taining 100 percent recovered waste paper, of which at least 20 percent is
postconsumer waste.

CONTENTS

EDITORS' NOTES

Although most of the work done in an institutional research office deals with numeric data, effective decision support often requires qualitative information that puts numeric information into the context of the decision to be made. New Directions for Institutional Research, numbers 34 and 72, present qualitative applications used in support of campus planning and decision making. The discussions in those monographs offered useful information about qualitative data collection and analysis methodologies. However, there was no attempt to compare or contrast the qualitative and quantitative paradigms. In addition, the authors of these earlier volumes did not recognize the potential strength of decision support that reflects an appropriate balance of quantitative and qualitative information.

The volume presented here attempts to integrate qualitative and quantitative information in decision support and decision making. Within the framework of systematic inquiry and effective decision support, we identify and illustrate the techniques and realities of creating, communicating, and using decision support information that reflects an appropriate balance of qualitative and quantitative data and information. From these discussions emerges an additional conclusion: maximizing the effectiveness of decision support requires that the institutional analysis function be located in close organizational proximity to institutional decision makers.

We begin with a two-chapter discussion that establishes a conceptual and theoretical framework and their application for the creation of evaluation information. In Chapter One, Kenneth W. Borland Jr. discusses, from a paradigmatic perspective, the nature and assumptions that dictate the selection of quantitative and qualitative methodologies and the generalizability of the information created through these complementary approaches to systematic inquiry.

In the second chapter, Josetta S. McLaughlin, Gerald W. McLaughlin, and John A. Muffo identify methodological procedures and techniques for creating decision support information that reflects the integration of qualitative and quantitative data. Applications of these techniques are illustrated with examples of data collection and analysis efforts conducted by institutional researchers in support of the assessment of an academic support function.

Chapter Three presents conceptual models that provide frameworks for the creation, formatting, and communication of effective decision support. Here Richard D. Howard describes components of effective decision support on a campus, presenting and discussing conceptual models that reflect different decision-making philosophies, decision support processes, and communication.

The following three chapters discuss the integration of qualitative and quantitative data in relation to the creation and communication of information by decision support functions and the information's use by decision makers. The authors of these chapters use both theory and examples of effective practice for balancing quantitative and qualitative information in their decision support and decision-making roles.

When communicating the results of a study to a decision maker, the institutional researcher must understand the context in which the decision is to be made and develop a report (oral, written, or visual) that provides the decision maker with information that reduces uncertainty. In Chapter Four, Marsha K. Moss discusses the reality of communicating information that reflects the appropriate balance of qualitative and quantitative information. Examples are used to illustrate how balancing these two types of information has been accomplished.

In Chapter Five, Ann S. Ferren and Martin S. Aylesworth discuss the management of academic affairs and the data and information support that can be provided by institutional research. Using examples of critical decisions that are routinely the purview of the provost and vice president for academic affairs, these authors describe qualitative and quantitative data and information that are necessary for effective management and evaluation of academic programs.

In Chapter Six, Mark L. Perkins discusses the role that appropriately balanced qualitative and quantitative information has played in his decision making. From his perspective as chancellor of the University of Wisconsin–Green Bay, Perkins identifies situations (1) where quantitative support is the driving force behind the decision, (2) where the qualitative aspects of the support drive the decision, and (3) where a balanced combination of the two types of information provide the most useful support.

In a slightly different but related look at the use of qualitative and quantitative information in support of institutional management and leadership, Jonathan D. Fife discusses the critical role of measurement in building institutional quality in Chapter Seven. Meeting the dynamic needs of stakeholders for institutional quality requires the continuous monitoring and analysis of the institution's inputs, processes, and outputs.

In the final chapter, we identify the main points developed in the preceding chapters and attempt to develop a conceptual model that reflects the balance of qualitative and quantitative information in decision support. This model integrates Terenzini's three tiers of intelligence (1993), the contextualization of data and information, and proximity of the institutional researcher to the decision maker. We end the chapter with some suggestions for the institutional research professional and the decision maker for enhancing the quality of decision support on the campus.

From our perspective, the decision support goal of institutional research has changed little since Peter Ewell edited the sixty-fourth issue of *New Directions for Institutional Research*: to reduce uncertainty in the decision making of managers and leaders on our campuses. As he indicated in the Editor's Notes of that volume, "Thinking about the issue [decision support] is the most important ingredient in addressing it. We hope that this volume will once again provoke practitioners to do so" (1989, p. 4).

Richard D. Howard
Kenneth W. Borland Jr.
Editors

References

Ewell, P. T. "Information for Decision: What's the Use?" In P. T. Ewell (ed.), *Enhancing Information Use in Decision Making.* New Directions for Institutional Research, no. 64. San Francisco: Jossey-Bass, 1989.

Terenzini, P. T. "On the Nature of Institutional Research and the Knowledge and Skills It Requires." *The Journal of Research in Higher Education,* 1993, 34(1), 1–10.

RICHARD D. HOWARD *is associate professor of adult and higher education at Montana State University–Bozeman.*

At the time of writing KENNETH W. BORLAND JR. *was assistant vice provost for academic affairs and assistant professor of adult and higher education at Montana State University–Bozeman. Currently he is associate provost at East Stroudsburg University.*

1

In spite of these very different approaches to creating knowledge, both qualitative and quantitative research paradigms reflect legitimate and valuable forms of disciplined or systematic inquiry that can result in stronger decision support than when used independently.[1]

Qualitative and Quantitative Research: A Complementary Balance

Kenneth W. Borland Jr.

The creation of knowledge, regardless of the context, requires the collection and analysis of data. Regardless of the specific form that this activity takes, quality knowledge will result only if the research process is systematic and follows the scientific method. *Research* has been classically defined as "the systematic and objective analysis and recording of controlled observations that may lead to the development of generalizations, principles, or theories, resulting in prediction and possibly ultimate control of events" (Best and Kahn, 1998, p. 18).

Within the past thirty to thirty-five years some have questioned the relevance of traditional empirical research, arguing that experimental designs create an artificial environment that results in artificial reactions or behaviors on the part of the participants. Qualitative research methods have been advanced as the only way to understand truth: to study the subject holistically rather than by controlling all of its aspects but one.

The relationship between qualitative and quantitative research should not be considered in terms of a mutually exclusive dichotomy but rather as a continuum of complementary paradigms within systematic scientific inquiry that, when used in concert, produce complete or useful knowledge. Although these two research paradigms are often compared and contrasted, I argue that the most useful research typically results from appropriately applying both research paradigms, strategically combining their traditional approaches and methodologies to create knowledge in support of decision making.[1]

In this chapter the characteristics of the qualitative and quantitative paradigms are discussed. Following this, a table is presented that identifies the primary components of systematic research, comparing traditionally classified qualitative and quantitative paradigms at each point in the

NEW DIRECTIONS FOR INSTITUTIONAL RESEARCH, no. 112, Winter 2001 © John Wiley & Sons, Inc.   5

research process. A concluding discussion presents the relevance of integrating both paradigms in the institutional research function to provide more powerful knowledge for decision making than would be generated by the use of any single approach.

Characteristics of the Qualitative Paradigm

The researcher must consider four philosophical questions and one practical question. The first of the former is, what is truth? Within the qualitative research paradigm, it is not only impossible to establish absolute truth, but relative truth is also bounded by the point in time and the place in which it is observed (that is, context) as well as by the perceptions of the respondents, researcher, peer reviewer, and consumer of the research.

The second philosophical question is, what is a human being? Aside from an answer focused on ethical concerns about control groups and experimentation, within the qualitative research paradigm the institutional researcher endeavors to observe human beings (as individuals and within systems or organizations) holistically rather than as sums of their parts. No one human factor can be understood outside of the entirety of its natural context and the perceptions that humans have of it.

The third philosophical question is, what is the role of the researcher? Institutional researchers who conduct qualitative research must recognize that they are the primary instruments for research design, data collection and management, data analysis, and the interpretation and reporting processes.[2] Researchers must be ever conscious that they could and often do influence every aspect of the research. Trustworthiness is at risk. Therefore, researchers are obligated to impose a design structure that increases levels of certainty about relative truth and to decrease subjectivity ("unreliable, biased, or probably biased") while increasing objectivity ("reliable, factual, confirmable, or confirmed").[3] This can be illustrated as seen in Figure 1.1.

In Figure 1.2, Howard and Borland (2000) present a model wherein the researcher structures to reduce subjectivity. Factual error is addressed and reduced via data verification with the respondents. The researcher asks

Figure 1.1. Subjectivity Reduction via Structural Increase

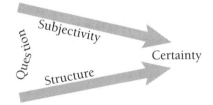

respondents if the recorded narrative data is what they said. Interpretation error is addressed and reduced via analysis verification with peer reviewers. Interpretation verification is provided as peer reviewers or auditors examine the researcher's coded field notes, transcripts, journals, artifacts and documents, and so on against an analysis provided by the researcher (Howard and Borland, 2000).

The final philosophical question is, what can qualitative research accomplish? Qualitative research is primarily descriptive—and in a limited way. Its contribution to systematic scientific inquiry is that rather than supplying a little detail about an entire population or category, it seeks to describe much detail about a few selected individuals or phenomena.

Six approaches to qualitative research serve to create knowledge. History is focused on the past. Biography is focused on the life of one person. Phenomenology examines the meaning of a human experience and the construction of meaning within the sample. Grounded theory seeks to develop a model or theory where none exists relative to the sample. Ethnography involves describing and interpreting one culture or group sample to another culture or group. Case study develops an in-depth analysis of a single organization, system, family, event, and so on or multiple cases wherein all of the possible internal and external relationships are considered: describing all possible relationships within the system.[4]

Qualitative research is well suited for two desired ends. It can be used to formally develop theories and models to be tested via quantitative

Figure 1.2. A Conceptual Model of Qualitative Research

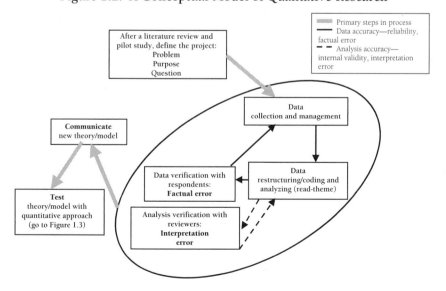

research, which is the first step in systematic scientific inquiry. Of course, these theories and models are tested quantitatively as the second step in systematic scientific inquiry. Qualitative research can also be used to explore the meaning that humans attach to quantitatively derived and tested conclusions, which is the third step in systematic scientific inquiry.

However, qualitative research is limited in terms of inferential power (generalizability). The researcher can more freely generalize if the sole consumer of the research report is also the sole object of the study. For example, institutional researchers who conduct a case study related to Greek life at their institution may generalize for that institution's research report consumers. They may not generalize for other institutions' consumers or regarding the Greek organizations that they did not study. Institutional researchers from other campuses as consumers of qualitative research will find the results of the report useful only to the degree that they judge their own human experience, context, and perceptions as similar to the environment in which the research was created.[5]

"Is it worth the time?" is a practical question about qualitative research that the institutional researcher must consider. Qualitative research yields valuable knowledge for decision makers. When conducted with appropriate levels of structure and a balance of objectivity and subjectivity to increase certainty, it provides theories, models, and descriptions of human experiences and perceptions within particular contexts. However, by its nature, qualitative research must be done in such a way as to provide rich-thick description. It takes a great amount of time on task (engagement) to produce the highest-quality qualitative research. Yet if decision makers need data that is contextually and humanly framed, qualitative research is the only means to that end. Institutional researchers may not be able to invest all the time necessary to produce the very best qualitative research, but they must compromise between rich-thick and quick-dirty time investments if they are to provide decision makers with valuable qualitative knowledge.

Characteristics of the Quantitative Paradigm

The purpose of quantitative research is to describe, predict, and control. In this type of research, specific variables are isolated through control of the environment (often through sampling techniques) to eliminate the effects of confounding variables and testing their relationship to various behaviors.

What Is Truth? In the most extreme sense of the quantitative paradigm, truth or reality is orderly, lawful, and predictable. Specifically, strict adherence to this paradigm assumes that all behaviors are predictable and that events occur consistently in relation to one another. As such, a cause-effect relationship exists that can explain any behavior, and this relationship can be used to predict or control behaviors if one is able to identify and collect the appropriate measures.

Who Is Studied? Using the quantitative paradigm, the institutional researcher does not study individual human beings but rather seeks to identify relationships between variables that explain behaviors that define specific populations of individuals. The keys are to accurately define the specific population of interest and to select a sample that accurately represents it. Sampling error, or not selecting a sufficiently representative sample, is one source of error in quantitative research and is recognized by the use of conditional or probabilistic parameters when inferring the applicability of the study's results from the sample to the population.

What Is Studied? An initial and critical component in quantitative research is for the institutional researcher to define variables that operationalize or reflect the constructs being studied. Once these measures have been operationally defined, instruments are created to record the measures (data) on the individuals being studied, and methodologies are developed to facilitate the collection of data. A primary concern in the development of the data collection instruments and methodology is to isolate specific behaviors and explore their hypothesized relationship to one or more variables of interest. This step in the process introduces a second source of error—measurement. Instruments and procedures designed to collect the data need to be pretested to establish their validity and reliability, both in terms of the content being measured and its applicability to the sample (population) being studied.

What Is the Role of the Researcher? The institutional researcher plans the study, including the design of the data collection instruments, data collection and management methodologies, and data analysis, in great detail before the start of the research process. Previous research often plays an important role in guiding the design. In conducting the research, each subject is studied in the same way in an attempt to eliminate bias that would create problems with the data analysis, interpretation, and generalizing to the population.

What Can Quantitative Research Accomplish? The primary purpose of quantitative research is the creation of knowledge by testing or confirming theory. Methods are designed that allow for the results and interpretations of quantitative research on representative samples to be inferred to the population under study within the bounds of a predetermined level of confidence. As such, institutional researchers never know in an absolute sense the accuracy of their inference. Consistency of results through replication and refinement of the study results in greater confidence about the truth of the findings as related to the population being studied. In Figure 1.3, a conceptual model is presented that illustrates a framework for conducting quantitative research that tests theories or models (Howard and Borland, 2000). Using such a framework, the findings from other studies can be tested for their meaning in regard to internal decision support issues or to test findings in external contexts to establish degrees of generalizability.

Figure 1.3. A Conceptual Model of Quantitative Research

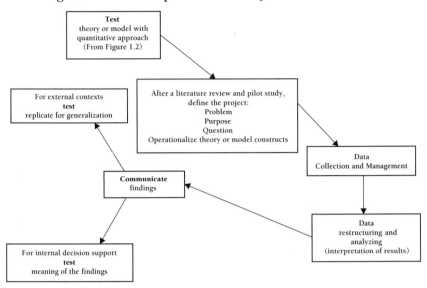

Although many approaches to quantitative research exist, they generally fall into the following categories. *Descriptive research* is intended to delineate the current status or condition of a population in relation to a specific set of variables. Two forms of descriptive research are *correlational research*, which investigates the mathematical relationship between two variables, and *causal-comparative research*, which attempts to identify reasons or causes for the current status or phenomena under study. *Experimental research* tests hypotheses about cause-effect relationships.

Quantitative research strategies are used primarily to test the truth of hypotheses or theories developed inductively in the first step of the scientific method.

Comparing, Contrasting, Complementing

Table 1.1 is a simplistic attempt to compare and contrast the qualitative and quantitative research strategies and their traditionally assigned attributes (Howard and Borland, 1999).

A compare-and-contrast approach, however, limits the researcher's understanding of systematic scientific inquiry. What is lost is the complementary relationship of qualitative and quantitative paradigms within systematic scientific inquiry. To illustrate this relationship, see Figures 1.2 and 1.3.When they are placed in proximity and considered together, one can more readily identify the exchange and flow between the paradigms. The qualitative generation of theory is to be quantitatively tested, and for researchers working within the context of the study, systematic scientific

Table 1.1. Comparing and Contrasting Qualitative and Quantitative Research Strategies

Qualitative	Quantitative
The purpose is to explain and gain insight and understanding of phenomena through intensive collection of narrative data.	The purpose is to explain, predict, or control phenomena through focused collection of numerical data.
Approach to Inquiry	
Inductive, value laden (subjective), holistic, process oriented.	Deductive, value free (objective), focused, outcome oriented.
Hypotheses	
Tentative, evolving, based on particular study.	Specific, testable, stated prior to particular study.
Review of Related Literature	
Limited; does not significantly affect particular study.	Extensive; does significantly affect particular study.
Research Setting	
Naturalistic (as is) to the degree possible.	Controlled to the degree possible.
Sampling	
Purposive: Intent to select small, not necessarily representative sample to acquire in-depth understanding.	Random: Intent to select large, representative sample to generalize results to a population.
Measurement	
Nonstandardized, narrative, ongoing.	Standardized, numerical, at the end.
Design and Method	
Flexible, specified only in general terms in advance of study. Nonintervention, minimal disturbance. All descriptive— history, biography, ethnography phenomenology, grounded theory, case study (hybrids of these).	Structured, inflexible, specified in detail in advance of study. Intervention, manipulation, and control. Descriptive— correlational, causal-comparative, experimental.
Data Collection Strategies	
Document and artifact collection. Observation (participant, nonparticipant). Interviews/focus groups ([un-]structured, [in-]formal). Administration of questionnaires (open ended). Taking of extensive, detailed fieldnotes.	Observation (nonparticipant). Interviews and focus groups (semistructured, formal). Administration of tests and questionnaires.
Data Analysis	
Raw data are words. Essentially ongoing, involves synthesis.	Raw data are numbers. Performed at end of study, involves statistics.
Data Interpretation	
Conclusions tentative, reviewed on an ongoing basis; generalizations speculative or nonexistent.	Conclusions and generalizations formulated at end of study; stated with predetermined degree of certainty.

inquiry comes full circle with the subsequent qualitative testing of the meaning of the numeric findings to persons within that context. Rather than the often-taken qualitative-versus-quantitative position, clearly the qualitative-and-quantitative perspective is more in keeping with systematic scientific research.

Relevance to Institutional Research

As identified in many of the publications describing and defining the role of institutional research, one of its primary purposes is to create information and knowledge to support planning and decision making. What have been described on the preceding pages of this chapter are two paradigms and their respective approaches for creating knowledge. Qualitative and quantitative research, when conducted in the isolation of their respective paradigms rather than in the context of systematic scientific inquiry, require the acceptance of diametrically opposed assumptions about the nature of reality. For example, the approaches for data collection and analysis traditionally associated with each of these paradigms can reflect contradiction when considered in isolation. Another example is that the primary responsibility for generalization rests with the researcher in a quantitative study, whereas the reader must make those decisions about the results of a qualitative study.

In spite of these very different approaches to creating knowledge, both research paradigms, when applied via strategies to reduce subjectivity and to increase levels of structure in the design, reflect legitimate and valuable forms of disciplined or systematic inquiry. Therefore, the relationship between qualitative and quantitative research should not be considered by institutional researchers as a mutually exclusive dichotomy but rather as a continuum within systematic scientific inquiry that is useful for decision support.

Notes

1. I distinguish between research paradigms, approaches, and methods. *Paradigms* are worldviews that ultimately cannot be proven. Researchers bring a paradigm to their research subject, and it determines, explicitly or implicitly, three things: epistemology (how the researchers know or claim to know), ontology (what the researchers know), and methodology (how the researchers will collect knowledge or data). For more on paradigms, see Lincoln and Denzin, 1994. *Approaches* are fundamental frameworks of research design that traditionally, following the type of research question asked, lead to particular research outcomes; for example, grounded theory, ethnography, causal-comparative, correlational, and so on. *Research methods* are means to collect, manage, and analyze data and are not limited to particular approaches. For example, interview, focus group, questionnaire, and others may be used within numerous research approaches.

2. The author distinguishes a variation of qualitative research known as *action research* in such a way as to remove it from a discussion of institutional research. Although in action research the researcher is the primary instrument for research design, data collection and management, data analysis, and the interpretation and reporting processes, the researcher is also the primary consumer of the research. Therefore, the action

researcher is the decision maker and action taker, and this is not the role of institutional researchers who provide decision support.

3. For a fuller discussion of this matter, Lincoln and Guba, 1985, chap. 11.

4. Cresswell (1998) provides a fuller description of biography, phenomenology, ethnography, grounded theory, and case study.

5. Debates within qualitative research circles regarding generalizability suggest a range of thought concerning inferential power afforded to the researcher. Again, see Lincoln and Guba, 1985, chap. 11; and Eisner and Alan Peshkin, 1990, pt. 3, in which Robert Donmoyer, Janet Ward Schofield, and Howard S. Becker consider generalizing from qualitative inquiry.

References

Best, J. W., and Kahn, J. V. *Research in Education.* (8th ed.) Boston: Allyn & Bacon, 1998.

Cresswell, J. *Qualitative Inquiry and Research Design: Choosing Among Five Traditions.* Thousand Oaks, Calif.: Sage, 1998.

Eisner, E. W., and Peshkin, A. *Qualitative Inquiry in Education: The Continuing Debate.* New York: Teachers College Press, 1990.

Howard, R., and Borland, K. "Qualitative and Quantitative Research in Institutional Research: Complementary or Competitive Paradigms and Methodologies?" Paper presented at the Association for Institutional Research 39th Annual Forum, Seattle, May 1999.

Howard, R., and Borland, K. "Assessment: A Qualitative Umbrella Shared by Action Research and Institutional Research." Paper presented at the Association for Institutional Research 40th Annual Forum, Cincinnati, May 2000.

Lincoln, Y., and Denzin, N. *The Handbook of Qualitative Research.* Thousand Oaks, Calif.: Sage, 1994.

At the time of writing KENNETH W. BORLAND JR. was assistant vice provost for academic affairs and assistant professor of adult and higher education at Montana State University—Bozeman. Currently he is associate provost at East Stroudsburg University.

2

Successful program evaluation may require identifying various studies that employ both quantitative and qualitative methodologies.

Using Qualitative and Quantitative Methods for Complementary Purposes: A Case Study

Josetta S. McLaughlin, Gerald W. McLaughlin, John A. Muffo

Consider the following scenario:

> Provost Gram has just left a message on your e-mail. Several groups and individuals are raising issues with her about what is being done in the institution to improve the ability of students to be successful. One of the most impressive and expensive initiatives by the institution over the last several years has been a program to enhance the effectiveness of mathematics instruction. Heavily involving computers and various forms of technology, the program has been a focal concern for those who would like to see the funds spent on other priorities.
>
> Provost Gram sets up a meeting with you and the chair of the mathematics department during which Provost Gram describes some of the pressures on the institution. The issues are framed through a series of generic questions: Is the program doing a good job? Is the program worth the money being spent on it? Should the program be continued? What should be changed to make the program more effective?

This scenario is not uncommon. Many issues debated by administrators in higher education are multifaceted and involve discussions about resources that must be allocated across many different and competing programs. The questions that need to be addressed are not always clearly delineated, and the complexity of issues often requires more than a simple study. Institutional researchers are thus challenged to refine and

NEW DIRECTIONS FOR INSTITUTIONAL RESEARCH, no. 112, Winter 2001 © John Wiley & Sons, Inc.   15

restate the issues so that useful information can be developed for decision makers.

The concerns that were expressed by Provost Gram can be addressed through the design of an effective program evaluation. Institutional researchers are faced with the realization that such evaluations are complicated by a number of factors. First, the evaluation often occurs as an afterthought. The institutional researcher must evaluate an ongoing program for which no carefully planned evaluation strategy was implemented during its development. Second, educators and researchers having an interest in the evaluation may not agree about the appropriateness of specific research designs for evaluating the program. Although many writers in the field of evaluation insist on the use of comparison groups as a control for individuals participating in the program, that is, the treatment group, others argue that the practical constraints in using an experimental research design necessitate the use of alternative, nonexperimental approaches to evaluation (Fitz-Gibbon and Morris, 1987). Third, political concerns dictate that the institutional researcher produce credible information geared for a diverse audience rather than just the individual who initially requested the evaluation. For example, in the scenario at the beginning of this chapter, Provost Gram asked for the evaluation; other groups interested in the outcomes of the evaluation would be members of the faculty, particularly the academic department directly involved in developing the program; external groups such as state and accrediting agencies; and students affected by the program's outcomes.[1]

In complex situations such as that just described, the institutional researcher's effectiveness will depend on his or her ability to define and delimit the concerns of the different audiences (Terenzini, 1993). To do so requires that the researcher be familiar with a broad array of methods that can use available data and create new data. In this chapter, we identify and discuss an evaluation strategy that meets this criterion. It uses multiple methods and embeds studies within a case study or program evaluation. The studies use qualitative and quantitative data to explore different but complementary questions important to the evaluation. Our rationale for implementing a strategy using multiple methods is that different groups need information generated through the use of different methods. Although one group may need information that is best developed utilizing quantitative methods, for example, predicted grades, a second group may need information that is best developed utilizing qualitative methods such as studies of student perceptions.

Building a Rationale for the Use of Multiple Studies

In the single-study evaluation, successful institutional research requires identification of the best study given the nature of the program evaluation, the rules of evidence held by the audience, and the questions being asked.

Single studies are appropriate in instances where just one focused question must be answered. However, when decisions about complex issues are being made, the single study usually does not adequately address the array of questions being asked by a diverse audience.

In cases where multiple questions are being asked, the appropriateness of using multiple studies and multiple research methods must be examined. The adequacy of a given method is a function of the researcher's ability to use that method to answer the questions being asked and to be able to persuade the end user that the method is credible. The choice of methods is complicated by differences in the characteristics of different audiences. Some prefer methods that produce numbers and graphs to describe outcomes. Others prefer methods that produce comments and opinions that lead to the development of concepts and ideas.[2]

Differences in preferred methods are generally believed to exist between disciplines. For example, accountants are frequently assumed to prefer the use of quantitative methods. As we associate accountants with cost-benefit studies, we might also associate philosophers with conceptual analyses, psychologists with statistical analyses, engineers with graphs, sociologists with case studies, and executives with executive summaries. Understanding the differences between disciplines is important because the audiences for program evaluation outcomes in higher education are likely to come from a number of different disciplines. Designing a program evaluation that incorporates a diverse array of techniques having appeal to the different groups may thus be the only practical means by which all pertinent information needs can be met.

Choosing a Research Strategy

Research designs incorporating more than one method are referred to as *multiple methods*. The concept itself is a common one in program evaluation (Mark and Shotland, 1987). It has various meanings, including but not limited to the use of multiple methodologies (Cook and Reichardt, 1979; Kidder and Fine, 1987) and use of multiple measures of a construct (Campbell and Fiske, 1959). The general idea underpinning multiple methods is that although "no single method is perfect," if different methods lead to the same answer, then "greater confidence can be placed in the validity of one's conclusions" (Shotland and Mark, 1987, p. 77). Over time, this idea has led to widespread advocacy of triangulation in the study of a given construct.

Triangulation is one of several models currently used in program evaluation, three of which are described by Mark and Shotland (1987). The models of multiple methods are the triangulation model, the bracketing model, and the complementary purposes model. Mark and Shotland (1987) point out that the idea underpinning the triangulation model is closest to that idea most frequently providing a rationale for use of multiple methods.

It is assumed that if one method converges across (other) methods on the answer, the result will be a single estimate that is more accurate than what would have occurred with only one imperfect model. For example, the overall difficulty of materials in a course could be evaluated by conducting three studies using three types of data: student opinions, student grades, and faculty evaluations. If the results of all three studies point to the same conclusion, then greater confidence can be placed in beliefs concerning the level of difficulty. The bracketing model differs in that it focuses on a range of estimates. The idea underpinning this model is that the results of different methods can be considered as alternative estimates of the correct answer. For example, a study of the performance in a college math course of those with high grades in high school math and those with low grades in high school math could be used to develop one estimate of the difficulty of the course materials. Similarly, a study of the performance in the same college math course of those with high Scholastic Aptitude Test (SAT) math scores and those with low SAT math scores could be used to develop a second estimate. A third study using an expert panel to assess the difficulty of the course materials could provide yet another estimate. The third study would represent an alternative estimate of course difficulty utilizing a different and widely accepted qualitative method of assessment. Ultimately, the researcher's goal is to develop a range of estimates within which the true score or estimate for level of difficulty should fall.

The third model, the complementary purposes model, tends to have more utility for institutional researchers. The idea underpinning this model is that one can use multiple methods, with each method performing a different but complementary function. The researcher may thus focus on different methods for alternative tasks to enhance the interpretability of results. A qualitative study may make the statistical results of a quantitative study more understandable and thus enhance the ability to communicate the results of the overall study. Similarly, a qualitative study as the primary vehicle may be supported with results from quantitative studies that clarify the narrative. For example, in the math course being used as an example, the students' high school grades and SAT scores could be used to assess the difficulty of the course content. Additional information can be sought through collection of qualitative data from students on their perceptions of the difficulty of the course and the degree to which they felt actively involved in the learning process. Data could be collected on faculty perceptions of the motivation of the students based on the amount of homework completed and on the coverage and difficulty of the class based on student performance on examinations. Qualitative data would in this case be used to address questions not easily addressed using quantitative data such as high school and college grades and SAT scores.

This last model differs from triangulation and bracketing in that the methods do not need to be independent. Mark and Shotland (1987) point out that a researcher trying to enhance interpretability will likely find independence to be dysfunctional. This point is well taken for researchers who have as their goal building a foundation for improving the program being evaluated and who are less focused on statistical aggregation of the data and generalization of the findings to settings outside the boundaries of the institution.

The complementary purposes model lends itself to adaptation under the embedded case methodology proposed by Yin (1989), a single-case study within which subunits (or in our case, studies) are embedded within the larger case. When the study design includes an embedded unit of analysis with numerous data points, Yin suggests that the appropriate analysis should first be conducted within the subunit and then augmented by some analytic technique to the level of the case itself. For example, in evaluating the math course, the researcher can identify multiple studies that address the questions concerning student performance and course difficulty. As one study, data can be collected from focus groups at various points in time such as before the course started, the first week of class, at midterm, at the end of the course, and two months after the completion of the course. Meta-analysis might then be used to look for common threads of thought that connected these discussions. By doing this type of analysis, the researcher is able to identify primary subgroups and explore their perceptions and performances.

A second study can focus on time management by students and can utilize quantitative data such as time spent on homework, time spent in class, and time spent in tutoring sessions. A third study can focus on difficulty of the course based on some established criteria. The results of these and other studies incorporated into the case study can be integrated and used to assess student performance outcomes and perceptions relative to the level of difficulty of course materials and the amount of time devoted to course work. This research strategy requires that the nature of the case be defined and that a primary research question be used as an umbrella under which all studies become relevant. For example, the primary research question might be, Given the level of difficulty of the course, what factors impact student outcomes?

The complementary purposes model and the embedded case design represent strategies that can enable institutional researchers to effectively design research that meets the information needs of a diverse audience. In addition, these strategies permit the institutional researcher to deal with nonlinear research activities. When designing research based on traditional, classical techniques, a specific sequence of events starts with the definition of the problem and the body of knowledge from prior research. However, the institutional researcher frequently begins with a heuristic iteration of a problem definition followed by identification of questions and issues and the collection of data to support efforts at decision making by administrators. After some initial interpretation, the researcher frequently must redefine the problem and adjust the scope of the study. The redefinition of issues in turn influences decisions concerning the types of data needed to provide for complex decision making. This time-based, nonlinear aspect of institutional research poses many of the same dilemmas faced by sociologists using grounded theory methodologies. Learning occurs on the part of the researcher during the course of conducting the study, and this learning must then be codified into understandings and beliefs that evolve as part of the research process.[3]

In summary, answering questions raised in a complex environment may require the development of a strategy that uses multiple methods. Analyzing the audience and the questions produces multiple foci. Addressing these foci requires use of a research strategy that utilizes complex models such as the complementary purposes and embedded case study models. Ultimately, the specific research methods needed to support decision making in complex environments may, out of necessity, encompass techniques utilizing both quantitative and qualitative data and techniques that are recognized as credible by a broad range of academic disciplines.

Example: The Virginia Tech Math Emporium

Use of multiple methods for program evaluation will be described using the embedded case study as a vehicle. The case example is the Math Emporium at Virginia Polytechnic University (Virginia Tech), an innovative pedagogical and technology-driven approach to teaching freshman mathematics. The evaluation was requested by the administration to determine whether the high cost of developing and operating the emporium was justified by the amount of learning that was occurring. Other concerns were whether the benefits of the program could be proven to outside skeptics and whether the emporium should be shut down and the resources reallocated. For researchers, these concerns could initially be restated in relatively simple (but complex) terms: Is the Math Emporium both effective and efficient with respect to student learning and resource allocation?

The next steps in developing a case study of the Math Emporium involved identifying the primary and secondary research questions. (See Figure 2.1.) Once that difficult task was accomplished, researchers could choose the appropriate qualitative or quantitative methods for answering each question. The characteristics and concerns of the audience needing the information also had to be factored into the choice of methods.

The primary audience for the evaluation of the Math Emporium was the provost, other senior administrators, faculty members in the math department, and students taking math courses. The audience also included faculty outside the math department who are concerned about math skills of their students; individuals interested in the balanced allocation of resources; individuals interested in integrating technology into learning; and last but not least, faculty and staff who are proponents of actively engaging students in learning. Clearly, no one analysis or study or methodology will be seen as persuasive by all of these groups.

Figure 2.1. The Case Model

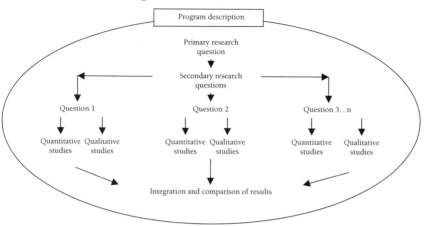

Case focus: Is the high cost of the program justified by the amount of learning that is occurring?

Primary research question: Is the Math Emporium efficient and effective with respect to student learning and resource allocation.

Secondary research questions:

1. Does instruction in the Math Emporium lead to improved student performance?
2. Does instruction in the Math Emporium result in high levels of student satisfaction?
3. Does instruction in the Math Emporium result in efficient use of resources?

Challenges: Getting Started

The challenge faced by researchers asked to evaluate the Virginia Tech Math Emporium was similar to that faced by many institutional researchers; they are too often called upon to evaluate a program ex post facto. Because recommended controls cannot be incorporated into the research design, the use of an experimental design as proposed by classical theoreticians is not an option. The institutional researcher must address issues by identifying a nonexperimental design that leads to credible research, the results of which are both confirmatory and diverse. If successful, the results of the study will provide a foundation for future evaluation efforts.

In our example, an embedded case study methodology that embeds both qualitative and quantitative methods developed ex post facto could be used to address questions about the effectiveness and efficiency of the Math Emporium. For example, both quantitative and qualitative studies of student learning and satisfaction could be conducted to produce estimates of effectiveness. Quantitative studies such as cost-benefit analysis and qualitative studies using expert panels could be employed to assess efficiency and allocation of resources. Each study ultimately chosen for inclusion should provide different but complementary information for decision makers.

The following sections provide examples that describe the use of quantitative and qualitative methods to examine learning and pedagogical effectiveness and student satisfaction with the Math Emporium. All studies were exploratory and were used as a starting point for development of future assessment instruments. As a caveat, no attempt is made to directly answer the question concerning the values associated with cost relative to student gains. Whether the gains in student learning justify the costs of developing the Math Emporium is a management judgment. Our job is to determine what the gains and costs were.

Choosing the Methodology

It has long been recognized that quantitative and qualitative methods produce different types of information.[4] The use of quantitative methods permits statistical analysis using standardized measures to measure and compare the reactions of a large number of people on a limited set of questions (Patton, 1997). By contrast, qualitative methods facilitate use of data that are perceived as rich, holistic, and real and for which face validity seems unimpeachable (Miles, 1983). These characteristics and the lack of standardization of much qualitative data make them difficult to analyze and require that the researcher devote much time and effort to managing the data.

In our example, the questions being asked required the use of both methods. Fortunately, a number of quantitative indices are generally available for use by institutional researchers, for example, grades in the Math Emporium, high school grades, SAT scores, and attendance records. A number of additional indicators can be developed by various means, including satisfaction scales and involvement indicators.

By contrast, qualitative indicators are less readily available. Developing a research design that incorporates collection of these indicators is important for a number of reasons. First, use of qualitative methods can lead to production of serendipitous findings. Second, use of qualitative methods can support decision makers who need to understand what people think, why people think what they think, and the values and motivations behind thought and behavior (Van Maanen, 1983; Patton, 1987). Third, when mixed, information developed using qualitative methods can be played against information from quantitative methods evaluating the same setting. The combination produces analyses that are more powerful than either method can produce alone (Miles, 1983).

In summary, studies embedded in the case study are chosen to provide different but complementary information for decision makers. The nature of the questions addressed determines the appropriateness of types of data collected. Quantitative methods utilize performance data to examine learning and pedagogical effectiveness while qualitative methods are used to collect data on student perceptions. All studies are exploratory and used as a starting point for development of future assessment instruments. A summary of studies is shown in Table 2.1.

Conducting the Research

Step 1: Describing the Program. One of the more important issues to remember in conducting research is that many audiences or end users will not have an adequate understanding of the program being evaluated. It was

Table 2.1. A Summary of Studies Embedded Within a Case Study of the Virginia Tech Math Emporium (ME)

Study	Contribution	Primary Tool	Method	Level of Analysis
Prediction of performance	Use prior performance to estimate effect of ME by class.	Complex statistical	Quantitative	Course/class
Comparison of grades	Compare grades in ME and prior to ME by class.	Simple statistical	Quantitative	Course/class
Student focus groups	Ask freshmen what they liked and how it might be improved.	Opportunity focus groups	Qualitative	Individual
Engineering student survey	Ask engineering students what they liked and how it might be improved.	Open-ended survey	Qualitative	Individual
Class notes	Describe classes and how taught and some of the results of activities.	Content analysis	Qualitative	Class
Expert visit	Look at ME and evaluate its worth and what might improve it.	Expert judgment	Qualitative	Organizational
Cost study	Identify major cost and attempt to compare to cost without ME.	Analytical accounting	Quantitative	Organizational
Literature review	Gather external evidence that increased involvement of engineer students in learning was better.	Literature review and secondary analysis	Qualitative	Theoretical

thus imperative that the evaluation report included a description of the Math Emporium in terms of facilities, the faculty resources involved, the equipment, the processes by which the students accessed the emporium, and so on. In the absence of a written description, information can be gathered through interviews with department heads, individuals in university facilities, and the faculty. A description of the Virginia Tech Math Emporium is presented in Appendix 2.1.

Step 2: Conducting the Study. Researchers must next identify those questions that can help direct the evaluation effort. The case of the Virginia Tech Math Emporium focused on whether the high cost of the program was justified by the amount of learning that was occurring. The primary research question was restated as follows: Is the Math Emporium efficient and effective with respect to student learning and resource allocation? Three secondary research questions were then formulated to provide direction for design of the subunits or studies:

1. Does instruction in the Math Emporium lead to improved student performance?
2. Does instruction in the Math Emporium result in high levels of student satisfaction?
3. Does instruction in the Math Emporium result in efficient use of resources?

STUDIES USING QUANTITATIVE METHODS. Two studies were designed using quantitative methods to address questions concerning the effectiveness of the Math Emporium with respect to student performance. The first study was a statistical analysis using regression to estimate the effect of taking mathematics in the Math Emporium. The second study was a direct comparison of student performance by course for the students who took mathematics at the Math Emporium versus those who had taken the same course during the preceding year in a more traditional setting.

Quantitative data used in this study are measures of academic performance readily available for use by institutional researchers. Regression analysis was used to model the academic performance of students in various mathematics classes. Actual grades from 17,069 first-time freshmen in seven courses were entered into a database along with measures of prior academic performance. The latter was measured using the student's math and verbal SAT scores; the student's class rank; final high school grade point average (GPA); overall average GPA among the student's high school English, math, science, humanities and social studies, and language courses; and the total numbers of these types of courses in which a student was enrolled from ninth through eleventh grade. This type of analysis of grades in a course is useful because it is generally believed that the students who participate in programs such as the Math Emporium will learn more if they are better prepared than other students in terms of mathematics. This requires controlling for the entering capability of the students, particularly where there is not random assignment. There was some evidence that entering students differed with respect to ability levels for the different years when measured by average high school grades and performance on the standardized mathematics achievement tests.

Effectiveness of the Math Emporium experience was examined relative to two measures—percentage of students successfully completing the course and average final grades received relative to pre-Math Emporium predecessors. Success was defined as making a grade of C or better. The analysis controlled for academic performance prior to enrollment in the math course taught at the Emporium, that is, the student's academic preparation and ability.

Effectiveness was first examined by developing logistic equations to model the probability that a student would succeed as a function of whether the course was taught in the Math Emporium (Kleinbaum, 1994). As noted previously, measures of the student's academic preparation and ability were incorporated into the model. The criterion of success used as the dependent variable for this model was whether the student received a grade of C or better for the course. Results are reported in Appendix 2.2.

Prior academic performance of students as measured by SAT scores and high school GPA was then used to best explain the actual grade that the student achieved in the math course. Least-squares regression was used to predict the grade. Grades were scored from 0 to 4, with F = 0, D = 1, C = 2, B = 3, and A = 4. The results are summarized in Appendix 2.3.

A second study using quantitative data was then designed to address some of the issues left unanswered by the first study. As noted previously, the results from the logistic regression analysis and the least-squares regression (Appendixes 2.2 and 2.3) were for a single semester. Although the statistical analysis allowed the researcher to make the adjustment for differing levels of student ability in the evaluation of the Math Emporium, it suffered from one major problem—it was difficult to explain and to interpret. This was particularly true for the logistics regression, where the impact of the emporium depended on the ability of the student. To overcome this limitation, a study was designed to make a direct comparison of grades that was more easily interpreted. The study compared students taking courses in the Math Emporium with students in more traditional classes the preceding year, the assumption being that both groups were similar in ability. Comparisons were done by course and by semester for academic year 1996–97 with grades for academic year 1997–98. The results are shown in Appendix 2.4.

The results for studies 1 and 2 generally support the belief that those students who received their math instruction using the Math Emporium showed improved performance relative to what would have otherwise been expected in the absence of instruction in this setting. In Study 1, improvement was significant for four courses—Math 1015, Math 1205, Math 1206, and Math 1224—when performance was defined by the likelihood of getting a grade of C or better in the course. This improvement was significant also for Math 1525 when one considers performance to be measured by the grade received in the course. In both cases, the Math Emporium seemed to have the least effect on student performance among the students of Math 1114, a course designed specifically for engineering majors. In Study 2, comparison of grades for two years tends to generally support the trend of improved performance by students receiving instruction through the Math Emporium.

STUDIES USING QUALITATIVE METHODS. The evidence of improved student learning found using quantitative methods did not provide information on student satisfaction with or perceptions of the Math Emporium. Put another way, statistical analysis of grade and past performance data did not completely meet the information needs of outcomes assessment. This is an important observation because pressures from audiences both internal to and external to institutions of higher education are increasingly defining student outcomes as more than the grade received. There is an interest in what the student learned and how that learning was applied. Furthermore, if administrators seek information that is rich and holistic and that informs them about what students think, it is imperative that these concerns be incorporated into the evaluative study. The institutional researcher will need to identify useful qualitative methods to meet these needs, especially in the short term, when reliable assessment instruments to measure satisfaction have not yet been developed.

A second concern is that although longitudinal studies had to be done to determine the long-term impacts of the Math Emporium on student learning, qualitative data were needed in the short term to lay the foundation needed to develop instruments for longitudinal research. A better understanding of student reaction to innovative pedagogy was also necessary for improvement of instruction within the lab setting. A final limitation to the statistical and numerical analyses was that they provided little information on what might have been done to improve the effectiveness of the Math Emporium.

A number of indices are available for use in program evaluation, including data from focus group interviews, faculty assessments, individual interviews, expert panels, and open-ended surveys. For our example, qualitative methods utilizing focus groups, open-ended surveys, and expert panels were used to assess student satisfaction with the Math Emporium.

Focus groups, or in-depth interviews, are among the most widely used qualitative research tools in the social sciences (Stewart and Shamdasani, 1990). They are almost always conducted with the collection of qualitative data as their primary purpose. Participants can qualify their responses or identify contingencies, thus producing a rich body of data. Furthermore, focus groups are more flexible, less costly, and quicker to implement than many other data collection strategies. The downside to using data collected from focus groups is that summarizing the data is often difficult and time consuming.

Despite these drawbacks, institutional researchers find that focus groups are particularly useful for program evaluations. Focus group techniques can be used to obtain general background information, to diagnose the potential for problems with new programs, and to generate impressions of programs. They are also useful for interpreting and adding depth to previously obtained quantitative results.

Participants in the focus groups organized to evaluate the Math Emporium were convenience samples, that is, students who were available in two freshmen residence halls and in classes for freshman student athletes. Two trained interviewers were present for each focus group. Three questions were asked of the focus groups: (1) What do you like about the Math Emporium? (2) What bothers you about the Math Emporium? (3) What do you suggest should be done differently? In addition to gathering data on student perceptions, evaluators wanted to collect opinions on how the Math Emporium might be improved.

Comments were transcribed and summarized. Partial results are shown in Appendix 2.5, with the top five comments summarized in order of importance by category of response. Some items have been combined for parsimony. Restructuring of comments in this way enables the researcher to identify areas or issues on which decision makers should focus their concerns.

Analysis of the qualitative data did in fact reveal areas of concern that are not obvious from the quantitative data. For example, students voiced high levels of satisfaction with the physical surroundings but low levels of satisfaction with the equipment and site location of the Math Emporium. Red flags were raised concerning relational factors when comments reflected student dissatisfaction with respect to the amount of teacher contact and types of student interactions occurring in the lab setting. The integrity of some students was questioned. The results also suggested that the students are concerned about efficient use of their time.

In general, the results from the third study contributed in two ways to the success of the program evaluation. First, the results added information that could be used by decision makers. Second, the results provided those insights needed to design an ongoing assessment of student satisfaction with the Math Emporium.

A second method for collecting the opinions and perceptions of individuals is the open-ended survey. This survey traditionally contains four or five general questions related to the topic of interest. Such surveys are very easy to construct but, like focus group interviews, are quite difficult to analyze and interpret.

The open-ended survey was administered to classes in the Department of Engineering Fundamentals. Given that most freshman engineering students take two mathematics classes per semester, distributing the surveys through those classes guaranteed that most of the students surveyed had experience with the Math Emporium, though normally in a small range of classes, that is, those required by the engineering curriculum. Because the results of the quantitative studies suggested that engineering students benefited less than other students from instruction in the Math Emporium, it was important to understand whether engineering students differed from the other student population in their perceptions of the Math Emporium.

Students were asked the following questions:

1. What do you *like* about the Math Emporium and your experiences there?
2. What do you *not like* about the Math Emporium and your experiences there?
3. What should be done differently at the Math Emporium?
4. Do you think that you learned more as a result of your experiences at the Math Emporium? (If yes, why? If no, why not?)

A random sample of 220 responses from students (179 males and 41 females) enrolled in four different math courses was analyzed. The top five responses to each question are shown in Appendix 2.6. As with focus groups, comments are summarized. However, the researcher has the added advantage when using a written survey of being able to more accurately record the frequency with which specific concerns are identified.

Results from questions 1, 2, and 3 are similar to the results from focus groups. There is no reason to believe, based on analysis of qualitative data, that engineering students were different in fundamental ways as may have been implied by the analysis of quantitative data. Their concerns were basically the same, for example, time management, convenience, usefulness of hardware and software, competence, and availability of tutors. Differences between engineering and other students were suggested by the results from question 4. Engineering students did not perceive that they learned more as a result of experiences at the Math Emporium, a perception that generally supported the statistical analyses in studies 1 and 2.

Data collected using focus groups and surveys should ultimately help the institution design interventions that will address concerns expressed by participants. The institutional researcher can assist by collecting additional data that support the need for interventions. A pedagogy that is consistent with the professional standards of the academic disciplines must be identified. An important source for ensuring that professional standards are met is the use of expert judgment.

Although faculty and administrators inside the institution where the program has been implemented represent one source of expert judgment, they may not be seen as credible by all audiences owing to their involvement in development of the program. A second source of expertise comes from faculty, administrators, and consultants from outside the institution. Their opinions represent usable data that is perceived as credible by many audiences. Experts are particularly useful for describing, analyzing, and interpreting the learning culture of a program such as that developing in Virginia Tech's Math Emporium. (Creswell, 1998, p. 67, discusses these and other types of qualitative studies.)

Experts invited to Virginia Tech to take part in the program evaluation engaged in the following activities: (1) discussions with students and faculty about what the students and faculty liked and did not like; (2) walks around the Math Emporium; and (3) observation of faculty, staff, and student activities. Their areas of expertise included mathematics and the processes of active learning and student engagement. The exit report provided opportunity for experts to engage key individuals from the university in a group discussion about the Math Emporium.

Results from discussions with students complemented and supported the results from the other qualitative studies of student perceptions. Discussions with the faculty concerning opinions about the learning process reinforced what the consultants observed and what the researcher identified. Results ultimately led to suggestions for interventions to improve the program.

Interviews conducted by experts provided the opportunity for faculty to discuss the implications of the Math Emporium with respect to expenditures and changes in department priorities. Experts also broadened the discussion to include issues of faculty support and priorities setting for future use of the Math Emporium.

Use of experts resulted in a series of comments and observations about the active nature of student learning. Their findings reinforced what had been inferred from student comments and from faculty class notes and assessments. Expert opinion thus attached credibility to the idea that the student should be involved in determining aspects of the learning process. The learning activities incorporated into the Math Emporium were identified as consistent with preferred pedagogical processes and as resulting in preferred learning from the viewpoint of the discipline. Expert opinion reinforced findings from the research literature on the benefits of experiential learning.

A number of studies should be conducted when evaluating a program that is competing for resources, including a cost study, faculty course assessments, and literature reviews. These were incorporated into the case study of the Virginia Tech Math Emporium but are not described here owing to space limitations.

Techniques for conducting the studies mentioned in the previous paragraph are well known. For the cost study, the major costs were identified in terms of equipment, personnel, and facilities, including lease payments or rents in addition to purchase costs. Where possible, costs attributed to the program were separated from costs associated with other activities. A number of questions concerning alternative costs were studied. For example, the following types of questions were asked: If the Math Emporium were not being used, how much would it cost to provide instruction as was previously done? If the computers had not been placed in the emporium, would they have been purchased for other uses? If an administrative unit such as Information Systems paid for the Math Emporium computers as part of its goal to meet objectives for classroom technology, is this a cost attributable to the Math Emporium? Can estimates of improvement in the number of students passing the course as a result of instruction in the Math Emporium be translated into the number of class enrollments that are saved by the new method, which can in turn be translated into classes, staff costs, and facility needs?

Similarly, the use of course notes from faculty who teach the courses for assessment is standard operating procedure in many institutions. The institutional researcher can ask that the notes be more detailed for purposes of the evaluation to include the specific procedure for using the emporium and additional insights from the faculty. In the example of the Math Emporium, faculty noted that "each student is expected to spend one hour in a classroom setting attending a focus group and three hours studying in the Math Emporium with the help of MATH 1015 staff. Staff are available 9:00 A.M. to midnight on Monday through Thursday and 9:00 A.M. to 4:00 P.M. on Friday as well as 4:00 P.M. to 11:00 P.M. on Sunday. Students are given credit toward the final grade for conscientiously doing these two activities. Although this may have led to better grades as a result, they also lost grade points for not showing up and signing in for these time periods." Examples of evaluative comments by the faculty about the effectiveness of the courses in supporting learning and in causing the active engagement of the students included the following: "A promising service to be provided by MATH 1015 and other courses in the future is down-the-line support for other courses, including those outside mathematics. If a student who has passed the course claims not to know something that is part of the curriculum, that student can be sent back to the Math Emporium. . . . This puts the responsibility to review such concepts on the students, with the Mathematics Emporium providing the services to make this possible."

Institutional researchers can also benefit from the use of results in previously published research on the issues being studied. Literature reviews can provide insights into questions being asked about the benefits of any program, especially one focusing on student learning and pedagogy. In our example of the Math Emporium, a previously funded study was identified that looked at the impact of increased engagement on the ability and motivation of the students, particularly engineering majors. Results, conducted with funding from the National Science Foundation, suggested that the long-term results of engagement for engineering students would likely be positive.[5] This finding, coupled with evidence from the research literature that active and collaborative learning activities enhanced student learning, implies that the long-term student learning of those using the Mathematics Emporium should be better than it would be under the more traditional lecture method to the extent that the courses using the facility encouraged student interaction with faculty and peers, hands-on activities with clear instructions, and appropriate structure.

Step 3: Integration and Interpretation of Results. The units of analysis for studies embedded within the case study vary as a function of the questions being investigated. Some studies focused at the individual level, whereas others focused at the class level. This provides a broad array of complementary information. The challenge for the institutional researcher is to identify a means for communicating the implications of the various studies for the program itself. The quality of institutional research rests on the degree to which it can meet this challenge and provide information that is relevant, sufficient, timely, and reliable. To accomplish this goal, data must be analyzed and the results then translated into useful information at the time that decisions are being made. In much the same way that theoreticians use mathematical equations and graphics to communicate their theory, institutional researchers can use matrices and graphics to communicate information drawn from multiple studies. Results and implications in table or matrix form can provide a visual map for the end user.

We will use the first four studies to demonstrate one possible approach. Table 2.2 is designed with the row headers indicating the study and the column headers indicating findings, consistencies/inconsistencies, and implications for the program.

Table 2.2. Integration and Interpretation of Results

Study 1	Study 2	Study 3	Study 4
		Findings	
Except for math for engineering students:

Instruction in the Math Emporium significantly increases the likelihood that students will succeed given past performance.

Instruction in the Math Emporium is associated with significantly higher grades. | When comparing two semesters (one before Math Emporium), there is a pattern of improvement, significant for some courses.

Pattern of improvement is not evident for engineering students. | Freshmen Participants:

Make no reference to improved performance.

Show resistance to new teaching approaches.

Give conflicting opinions about tutors.

Express concern about time and lab location.

Seem to dislike group work.

Are sensitive to hardware problems. | Engineering students:

Do not believe they have learned more through use of Math Emporium.

Express satisfaction with the physical learning environment.

Are positive about group work.

Express concern about skill level of tutors.

Express concern about time and lab location.

Dislike choices of hardware. |
| | | Consistencies/inconsistencies | |
| Findings generally supported by Study 2 on overall performance and by studies 2 and 3 on outcomes for engineering students. | Consistent with findings for studies 1 and 4. | Inconsistencies exist if one assumes that better performance translates to higher levels of satisfaction.

Inconsistency between engineering students in Study 4 and those in this study on usefulness of group work. | Consistent with studies 1 and 2 on usefulness of Emporium for engineering students. |

Summary

The studies chosen for the embedded case study demonstrate how to meet the needs identified for the program evaluation. First, quantitative methods can be used to estimate and predict performance and to describe costs. Second, qualitative methods can be used to describe the structure of and satisfaction with the program. Third, studies using qualitative and quantitative methods can be compared to look for confirmation and contradictions in findings. The embedded case study thus allows the researcher to move from identification of questions to usable information for decision making at the program level.

Students, faculty, and administrators were the primary audiences for the results of the studies. At the same time, these groups acted as primary data sources for the program evaluation. Though studies embedded in the case had limitations in terms of reliability and validity, a comprehensive assessment of the Math Emporium did emerge. This was made possible by comparing and contrasting results of different studies using different methods. By bringing together various methodologies and by building on what others have learned, information emerged that effectively assisted and supported decision processes in the institution.

In summary, successful institutional research requires identifying the various studies that are appropriate given the nature of the program evaluation, the rules of evidence held by the audience that is listening, and the questions being asked. The strengths of various methodologies should thus be examined during the design phase of the research effort. The answer to one question may require use of qualitative methodologies, for example, student perspectives on effectiveness of a computer lab setting, whereas quantitative methodologies may be more appropriate in other instances, such as cost effectiveness of the program. In addition to the design phase of the project, the appropriateness of various studies and methodologies will need to be continuously considered and reconsidered as the project continues. This continuous assessment is particularly important when key audiences change and when surprising facts are discovered.

Notes

1. A related issue is whether the institutional researcher has a clear understanding of the role he or she should play. It could be either as a summative evaluator or a formative evaluator. Individuals in top administrative positions may want to know whether the program obtained its overall goals, and thus the role of the institutional researcher would be that of a summative evaluator. By contrast, faculty may see the evaluation as a progress check being conducted during the course of the program, and thus the role would be that of a formative evaluator. (See Morris, Fitz-Gibbon, and Lindheim, 1987, for a description of summative and formative evaluations.) The summative evaluation must be designed with close attention to stated performance objectives. The formative evaluation requires less rigid data collection and is generally more flexible with respect to requirements of the research.

2. Individuals who have these predispositions tend to be found in specific disciplines and in certain roles. At a popular level, this differentiation has been described in various books such as those about Myers-Briggs types and the differences in the behaviors, values, and beliefs of these different types (Myers and Myers, 1990) At a more scholarly level, the audience's ability and willingness to be persuaded has been related to "attention factors, message quality, a person's involvement in the issue, and a person's ability to process persuasive argument." (Jowett and O'Donnell, 1992, p. 137). In other words, each person will have a different ability to learn from the various alternative methodologies, and the results of the various studies will be given different credibility by different individuals. In addition, each person will have a different motivation to learn from the various methodologies. Intuitively, using the preferred methodology of the audience will increase the likelihood that the members of that audience will accept the methodology as persuasive and accept the results as legitimate.

3. Selection of methodologies in the tradition of grounded theory (see Glasser and Strauss, 1967; Strauss and Corbin, 1994) is done with the understanding that the set of beliefs, or the theory, that initially drive the study will be changing as the research is being conducted. The researcher is expected to revisit the theory, modify it, and then modify the research to address the newly identified issues. The refinement of the beliefs and the methodology often come from interacting with those who are important to the

use of the results. It can also come from the discovery of related research that one finds as one moves through the major issues.

4. Patton (1987, p. 64) notes that the "ideal-typical qualitative methods strategy consists of three parts: (1) qualitative data, (2) naturalistic inquiry, and (3) inductive content or case analysis," whereas "the classic hypothetico-deductive approach would ideally include (1) quantitative data, (2) experimental (or quasi-experimental) research designs and (3) statistical analysis based on deductively derived hypotheses."

5. In a survey of 480 undergraduate engineering students at six other universities on knowledge and skills required by the Accreditation Board for Engineering and Technology, the authors concluded that opportunities to interact with faculty and to work collaboratively with peers in a classroom setting should lead to gains in professional competencies (Cabrera, Colbeck, and Terenzini, 1998).

References

Cabrera, A. F., Colbeck, C. L., and Terenzini, P. T. "Teaching for Professional Competence: Instructional Practices that Promote Development of Group, Problem-Solving, and Design Skills." Paper presented at the meeting of the Association for the Study of Higher Education, Miami, Fla., November 1998.

Campbell, D. T., and Fiske, D. W. "Convergent and Discriminant Validation by the Multitrait-Multimethod Matrix." *Psychological Bulletin*, 1959, *56*, 81–105.

Cook, T. D., and Reichardt, C. S. (*eds.*). *Qualitative and Quantitative Methods in Evaluation Research*. Thousand Oaks, Calif.: Sage, 1979.

Creswell, J. W. *Qualitative Inquiry and Research Design: Choosing Among Five Traditions.* Thousand Oaks, Calif.: Sage, 1998.

Fitz-Gibbon, C. T., and Morris, L. L. *How to Design a Program Evaluation.* Thousand Oaks, Calif.: Sage, 1987.

Glasser, B., and Strauss, A. *The Discovery of Grounded Theory.* Chicago: Aldine, 1967.

Jowett, G. S., and O'Donnell, V. *Propaganda and Persuasion.* (2nd ed.) Thousand Oaks, Calif.: Sage, 1992.

Kidder, L. H., and Fine, M. "Qualitative and Quantitative Methods: When Stories Converge." In M. M. Mark and R. L. Shotland (eds.), *Multiple Methods in Program Evaluation.* New Directions for Program Evaluation, no. 35. San Francisco: Jossey-Bass, 1987.

Kleinbaum, D. G. *Logistic Regression.* New York: Springer, 1994.

Mark, M. M., and Shotland, R. L. "Alternative Models for the Use of Multiple Methods." In M. M. Mark and R. L. Shotland (eds.), *Multiple Methods in Program Evaluation.* New Directions for Program Evaluation, no. 35. San Francisco: Jossey-Bass, 1987.

Miles, M. B. "Qualitative Data as an Attractive Nuisance: The Problem of Analysis." In J. Van Maanen (ed.), *Qualitative Methodology.* Thousand Oaks, Calif.: Sage, 1983.

Morris, L. L, Fitz-Gibbon, C. T., and Lindheim, E. *How to Measure Performance and Use Tests.* Thousand Oaks, Calif.: Sage, 1987.

Myers, I. B., with Myers, P. B. *Myers-Briggs Type Indicator: Gifts Differing.* Palo Alto, Calif.: Consulting Psychologists Press, 1990.

Patton, M. Q. *How to Use Qualitative Methods in Evaluation.* Thousand Oaks: Calif.: Sage, 1987.

Patton, M. Q. *Utilization-Focused Evaluation: The New Century Text.* Thousand Oaks: Sage, 1997.

Shotland, R. L., and Mark, M. M. "Improving Inferences from Multiple Methods." In M. M. Mark and R. L. Shotland (eds.), *Multiple Methods in Program Evaluation.* New Directions for Program Evaluation, no. 35. San Francisco, Calif.: Jossey-Bass, 1987.

Stewart, D. W., and Shamdasani, P. N. *Focus Groups: Theory and Practice.* Applied Social Research Methods Series, no. 20. Thousand Oaks, Calif.: Sage, 1990.

Strauss, A., and Corbin, J. "Grounded Theory Methodology: An Overview." In N. Denzin and Y. Lincoln (eds.), *Handbook of Qualitative Research.* Thousand Oaks, Calif.: Sage, 1994.

Terenzini, P. T. "On the Nature of Institutional Research and the Knowledge and Skills It Requires." *Research In Higher Education,* 1993, 34(1), 1–10.

Van Maanen, J. "Reclaiming Qualitative Methods for Organizational Research: A Preface." In J. Van Maanen (ed.), *Qualitative Methodology.* Thousand Oaks, Calif.: Sage, 1983.

Yin, R. K. *Case Study Research: Design and Methods.* Applied Social Research Methods Series, no. 5. Thousand Oaks, Calif.: Sage, 1989.

JOSETTA S. MCLAUGHLIN is director, School of Management and Marketing, Roosevelt University.

GERALD W. MCLAUGHLIN is director of institutional planning and research at DePaul University.

JOHN A. MUFFO is director of undergraduate assessment at Virginia Polytechnic Institute and State University.

Appendix 2.1. Description of the Math Emporium

The Math Emporium was first opened for classes on August 25, 1997. The purpose of the emporium was to provide a computer-based learning environment for instruction in selected freshman- and sophomore-level mathematics courses. The goals developed for the emporium were to improve student performance and to improve retention in math and math-related majors such as engineering. Courses covered by the Math Emporium included calculus, linear algebra, vector geometry, geometry, and computing for teachers. The math department cooperated with other departments in the development of courses. For example, Math 1114 was developed in cooperation with the College of Engineering, whereas Math 1525 was designed to meet the needs, including software suitability, of students from several departments.

The Math Emporium was open twenty-four hours a day, seven days a week. The facility provided 76,000 square feet of space, 17,000 of which were set aside for Information Services, an administrative unit. The furnishings included 500 computer stations arranged in pods of 6 with minimum use of partitions. There were one large lecture area; two enclosed classroom computer labs; two lounge areas; and partitioned spaces for a tutoring lab, staff offices, and small group sessions.

A math support staff made up of faculty members, graduate teaching assistants, and undergraduate assistants was available from 9 A.M. to midnight Monday through Thursday, from 9 A.M. until 4 P.M. on Friday, and from 4 P.M. until 11 P.M. on Sundays. Tutorial help was available from 6 P.M. to 9 P.M. Sunday through Thursday.

APPENDIX 2.2. RESULTS OF A STUDY OF

STUDENT PERFORMANCE IN THE VIRGINIA

TECH MATH EMPORIUM

Results indicate that for Math 1015, Math 1205, Math 1206, and Math 1224, instruction at the Math Emporium significantly increased the likelihood that a student would succeed in the course, given the effects on student success of the student's prior academic performance. Instruction at the Math Emporium also appeared to increase the likelihood of student success for the remaining three courses, but the increase was not substantial enough to be statistically significant. Notably, the course for which the Math Emporium mode of instruction seemed to make the least difference in student performance was Math 1114, a course specifically designed for engineering majors. Thus, the typical characteristics and general math ability of the students in this course likely differed from those of the students in the other courses. In addition, students in Math 1114 spent the least amount of time in the Math Emporium, and those fewer assignments could likely have led to the lower impact.

Some key results from this analysis are presented in Table A.1.

Information under "Change without Emporium" shows by what percentage a representative student's likelihood of succeeding would have been reduced if the student had not been instructed at the Math Emporium. For the purposes of this comparison, a representative student was defined as a student of a Math Emporium course for whom the likelihood of succeeding was equal to the proportion of Math Emporium students in the sample who received a satisfactory grade in that course. The column "Percent Success without Emporium" shows what the probability of success in the math course would have been for a representative student if instruction had not been at the Math Emporium but rather had followed more traditional methods.

The final column, "Unsuccessful Representative Students," uses the previous information to estimate how many additional representative students, out of a total number of students as given in the second column, most likely would not have received a satisfactory final course grade if the course had not been taught in the Math Emporium. For Math 1205, approximately 139 additional students would not have been successful (that is, they would have received a grade of C or lower). Among all of the classes evaluated, 45 additional representative students on average would have performed unsuccessfully in each course if it had not been taught using the Math Emporium. Among courses for which the Math Emporium was found to have a signif-

Table A.1. Effect of Math Emporium on Percentage of Students Receiving a C or Better

Course Number	N^a	Coefficient[b]	p-value	Percentage of Success with Emporium[c]	Change without Emporium[d]	Percentage of Success without Emporium	Unsuccessful Representative Students[e]
1015	949	0.5489	0.0001	81.85	8.15	73.70	77
1016	317	0.3211	0.2148	85.49	3.98	81.51	13
1114	1365	0.0010	0.9915	70.72	0.02	70.70	1
1205	1260	0.6908	0.0001	80.13	11.00	69.13	139
1206	389	0.4446	0.0409	82.82	6.33	76.49	25
1224	421	0.6531	0.0024	86.46	7.65	78.81	32
1525	784	0.1972	0.1666	80.15	3.14	77.01	25
Average	783.57	0.4081	0.2023	81.09	5.75	75.34	45

[a]The number of first-time freshmen in the sample that took the course at the Math Emporium.

[b]The coefficient for the Math Emporium effect from the logistic regression equation.

[c]The percentage of students in the sample who received a grade of C or better.

[d]The estimated reduction in the likelihood of receiving a satisfactory grade in the course was calculated as follows:

$$\Delta(\%) = \beta * prob * (1 - prob) * 100\%$$

where $\Delta(\%)$ = the percentage change in the likelihood of a satisfactory grade
    β = the coefficient for the Math Emporium effect,
    and prob = the prior probability or likelihood that the student would be successful in the math course

[e]How many additional representative students, out of a total number of students as given in the second column, most likely would not have received a satisfactory final course grade if the course had not been taught in the Math Emporium.

icant impact, this average number of representative students affected increases to 68. For all seven courses combined, the total number of representative students who were estimated not to have received a satisfactory math grade during the semester if instruction had utilized more traditional methods was 310. Note that these results were for a single semester.

APPENDIX 2.3. PERFORMANCE IN MATH

EMPORIUM CONTROLLED FOR PAST

PERFORMANCE

The results shown in Table A.2 indicate that instruction in the Math Emporium was associated with a significantly higher grade in five courses (Math 1015, Math 1205, Math 1206, Math 1224, and Math 1525). Significant improvements ranged from about .15 in Math 1015 to more than one-third of a letter grade in both Math 1206 and Math 1224. The average improvement for all courses was about .19 of a letter grade, and for the five courses where the improvement was significant, the average anticipated grade was .32 higher, representing an improvement of about 10 percent in the average grades. Once again, the Math Emporium showed the least effect among students of Math 1114, the course designed for engineering majors.

Table A.2. Effect of Math Emporium on Grades in Different Mathematics Courses

Course	N	Coefficient[a]	p-value	Average Grade	Average Grade Without Emporium
1015	949	0.1491	0.0027	2.56	2.41
1016	317	0.1165	0.1483	3.10	2.98
1114	1365	−0.0619	0.1557	2.33	2.39
1205	1260	0.2080	0.0001	2.53	2.32
1206	389	0.3904	0.0001	2.90	2.51
1224	423	0.3411	0.0001	3.00	2.66
1525	784	0.1817	0.0014	2.74	2.56
Average	783.57	0.1893	0.0441	2.74	2.55

[a]Note that all of the coefficients in this table describe the effects of the Math Emporium mode of instruction on students' success in these math courses given the effects of the numerous other predictors of student performance, including SAT scores and high school GPA. Thus, multicollinearity is a potential problem that would complicate the interpretation of the coefficients of individual regressors. To control for this possibility, a battery of multicollinearity diagnostic tests were performed on the data. No evidence of any problems with multicollinearity was detected.

APPENDIX 2.4. DIFFERENCES IN MATHEMATICS GRADES AFTER INSTITUTING THE MATHEMATICS EMPORIUM

The results shown in Table A.3 suggest a pattern of improvement, some of which was significant, when comparing across two fall semesters. Change was not always in the desired direction for the two spring semesters. The results shown in Table A.4 reveal that for fall 1997, over three hundred fewer students received grades of F in basic mathematics courses than did in fall 1996. Approximately five hundred fewer, equivalent to 10 percent of

Table A.3. Summary of Mathematics Grades, 1996–97 Versus 1997–98

Class	Math Courses	Number	Mean	95% Range		Number	Mean	95% Range
1015	Fall 1996	1384	2	0.07	Spring 1997	235	1.52	0.15
1015	Fall 1997	1137	2.44***	0.07	Spring 1998	177	2.14***	0.2
1016	Fall 1996	593	2.44	0.11	Spring 1997	1298	2.55	0.07
1016	Fall 1997	620	2.58	0.1	Spring 1998	1094	2.46	0.07
1114	Fall 1996	1595	2.36	0.07	Spring 1997	637	2.61	0.1
1114	Fall 1997	1580	2.3	0.06	Spring 1998	557	2.31***	0.1
1205	Fall 1996	1344	2.28	0.07	Spring 1997	277	2.07	0.15
1205	Fall 1997	1347	2.46*	0.06	Spring 1998	194	2.02	0.18
1224	Fall 1996	711	2.13	0.1	Spring 1997	1043	2.13	0.07
1224	Fall 1997	726	2.44***	0.1	Spring 1998	1138	2.12	0.07
1525	Fall 1996	972	2.38	0.08	Spring 1997	243	1.97	0.19
1525	Fall 1997	886	2.63***	0.08	Spring 1998	152	2.18	0.21
1526	Fall 1996	194	2.42	0.18	Spring 1997	733	2.44	0.1
1526	Fall 1997	200	2.1	0.18	Spring 1998	756	2.59	0.08
1614	Fall 1996	47	3.43	0.18				
1614	Fall 1997	44	3.78*	0.14				
1624					Spring 1997	44	3.46	0.15
1624					Spring 1998	47	3.63	0.17

*Significant at the .05 level.

***Significant at the .001 level.

Table A.4. Summary of D and F Grades, 1996–97 Versus 1997–98

Class	Semester	Number	Percentage of F's	Difference in Numbers	Percentage of D's and F's	Difference in Numbers	Semester	Number	Percentage of F's	Difference in Numbers	Percentage of D's and F's	Difference in Numbers
1015	Fall 1996	1384	18	102	34	171	Spring 1997	235	22	11	52	44
1015	Fall 1997	1137	9		19		Spring 1998	177	16		27	
1016	Fall 1996	593	13	25	24	19	Spring 1997	1298	8	-11	18	-22
1016	Fall 1997	620	9		21		Spring 1998	1094	9		20	
1114	Fall 1996	1595	13	63	24	0	Spring 1997	637	8	-22	19	-17
1114	Fall 1997	1580	9		24		Spring 1998	557	12		22	
1205	Fall 1996	1344	12	94	25	121	Spring 1997	277	15	-4	32	2
1205	Fall 1997	1347	5		16		Spring 1998	194	17		31	
1224	Fall 1996	711	15	22	31	65	Spring 1997	1043	12	11	30	23
1224	Fall 1997	726	12		22		Spring 1998	1138	11		28	
1525	Fall 1996	972	11	35	33	142	Spring 1997	243	27	17	39	17
1525	Fall 1997	886	7		17		Spring 1998	152	16		28	
1526	Fall 1996	194	11	-8	21	-18	Spring 1997	733	11	38	22	45
1526	Fall 1997	200	15		30		Spring 1998	756	6		16	
1614	Fall 1996	47	0	0	0	0						
1614	Fall 1997	44	0		0							
1624							Spring 1997	44	0	0	0	0
1624							Spring 1998	47	0		0	
Net difference				333		500				40		92

the freshman class, earned grades of D or F. This comparison thus supports findings of improved performance suggested by the two previous analyses. Though this study does not adjust for previous ability, the trade-off is that it is much easier to explain than the earlier regression studies and therefore more persuasive to the less statistically inclined end user.

Appendix 2.5. Summary of Results from

Focus Group Interviews

What do you like about the Math Emporium?

Access/Convenience	• Open twenty-four hours per day, seven days a week.
	• Tutors are helpful, available much of the time, and free.
	• Easy to schedule lectures.
	• Can go through quizzes before taking a test.
	• Flexible; self-pacing.
Aesthetics	• Comfortable chairs.
	• Air-conditioned.
	• Quiet; a good place to study any subject.

What bothers you about the Math Emporium?

Location	• Inconvenient; getting there is a big effort that wastes a lot of time.
	• Too far to go to accomplish what can be done in one's room.
	• Bus system is not timely; they are infrequent later at night; sometimes one has to walk home in the dark late at night.
	• Only reason to go there is to take tests on computers.
Hardware/Software	• System crashes frequently.
	• Server freezes while taking a test with incorrect point adjustment afterwards; better system needs to be developed in the interest of fairness.
	• Inefficient system; only Macs are used there; we are required to purchase PCs.
	• The Macs are slow or not preferred, and some don't have PC crossover option.
	• Cannot save without a disk; trouble with disk compatibility.
Employees	• Tutors are not helpful (twice as many responses as "are helpful" above).
	• Cups used to signal for help result in an inefficient system.
	• Coaches Corner not helpful.
	• Independent learners can do well there, but they are in the minority.
Dehumanization	• Removes teacher-student relationship.
	• Does not allow for human interaction.
	• Preference for teacher; paying money for academic credits without a real teacher.
	• Don't like doing math on a computer.
Group work/labs	• Partners trade off, rotating through assignment.
	• Pick up labs for a friend and complete them in the residence hall room.
	• Not effective—less retention.
	• Difficult to get several computers or chairs together for a work group.
	• Assigned to a group but would rather pick them oneself.

Cheating/security
- Weak guidelines; it's easy to cheat.
- Cheating goes on; people work together and/or use calculators.
- Sneak out of the building while supposed to be putting in required hours.
- Nobody knows if you are at your computer or not.
- Someone else can take your test.

What do you suggest should be done differently? How might it be improved?

General
- Make its use voluntary.
- Correct problems of computers locking up.
- The time required should be appropriate to the assignment.
- Schedule classes at the same times so that help can be solicited from classmates.

Employees
- Hire better or more helpful tutors.
- Hire more tutors.
- Develop a better way to signal for assistance.
- Tutors need to know more about math as well as computers.

Courses
- Allow students to do the work in their rooms.
- Offer some courses at the emporium and in traditional classrooms; provide a choice.
- Make MATH 1525 optional.
- Optional hours; no requirements for number of hours at the emporium.
- More advanced courses (such as calculus) should not be at the emporium.

Convenience/location
- Move the emporium to campus; move it to a more convenient location.
- More convenient bus schedule.
- Adjustable chairs.
- Have coin-operated copiers available.
- Have small sections of the emporium set up for quizzes.

Tests
- Allow calculators.
- Change the way each question is timed equally.
- More time allowed per question.
- Create a way to give partial credit.
- Ability to check each test when completed before submitting it.

APPENDIX 2.6. OPEN-ENDED RESPONSES

FROM ENGINEERING STUDENTS

Questions and Responses	No.

What do you like about the Math Emporium and your experiences there?

• It is a learning environment, a good place to study and do group work.	65
• The staff are friendly and helpful.	46
• Lectures and tutoring are available there.	43
• The chairs and computer arrangements are comfortable.	35
• It is open twenty-four hours a day seven days a week.	26

What do you not like about the Math Emporium and your experiences there?

• It is distant from campus, inconvenient to reach, and requires substantial travel time.	93
• There are hardware and software problems.	82
• The staff are not knowledgeable and are sometimes slow when there is a problem.	63
• Macs are used, but I own a PC or PCs elsewhere.	35
• It's a requirement to go there, so many hours are required, and checking in and out can take a lot of time.	35

What should be done differently at the Math Emporium?

• Get rid of the Macs and replace them with PCs; get better computers.	40
• The staff could be more helpful, especially in relation to certain courses and software being used.	39
• There should be better and more reliable hardware (especially servers), software, and printers.	33
• Make use of the emporium optional. Assignments can be completed elsewhere, often in one's room using the computer required by the university.	29
• There should be more tutors and other staff available over more hours.	24

Do you think that you learned more as a result of your experiences at the Math Emporium? If yes, why? If no, why not?

• No.	116
• Yes.	81
• I can learn the material just as well at home.	53
• I was forced to learn the material using the quick tests and interviews.	26
• It is a good place to get help and to meet with a group; the staff are helpful.	23

3

Although decision support can take many forms and reflects various levels of analytic complexity, its primary objective should be to reduce the decision maker's uncertainty.

Conceptual Models for Creating Useful Decision Support

Richard D. Howard

Although the day-to-day activities in an institutional research office reflect the specific needs, culture, and interests of its institution, a common characteristic across all institutional research offices is the creation of information to support decision making across their campuses. Decision support may take many forms and reflect various levels of analytic complexity. In spite of the different forms that decision support might take, its primary purpose is to reduce the decision maker's uncertainty in planning and other decision-making activities. Many authors have discussed and presented different techniques for developing and delivering effective decision support. Although these efforts have provided important technical and strategic guidelines for generating effective decision support information, they tend to provide situation-specific advice or technical models and analytic methodologies.

Senge (1990) introduced the notion of mental models as one of the five disciplines present in a learning organization. Mental models are "the images, assumptions, and stories which we carry in our minds of ourselves, other people, institutions, and every aspect of the world" (Senge and others, 1994, p. 235). This definition implies that mental models are extremely complex entities that exist in our minds to help us make sense of our environment. They provide a standard or template that allows an individual to compare what is observed to what should be. Describing or diagramming a mental model in its entirety is virtually impossible owing to the complexity of the human brain and its ability to absorb and analyze multiple issues and the complexities of their interactions. However, it is critical that individuals communicate the essence of their mental models so that complex processes, structures, and values can be consistently understood by all. This communication

NEW DIRECTIONS FOR INSTITUTIONAL RESEARCH, no. 112, Winter 2001 © John Wiley & Sons, Inc.

is usually done through the creation of a conceptual model that operationalizes the essence of the mental model. Conceptual models often take the form of a diagram or table, but they can also be developed through a narrative discussion and are much less complex than the mental models they represent.

In this chapter the issues of creating and communicating useful decision support are addressed through the presentation and discussion of conceptual models that have been developed over the past twenty-five years and presented at the Association for Institutional Research (AIR) Annual Forums or published in academic journals or books. These models reflect the work of many individuals, including institutional research professionals. It is my hope that the conceptual models presented in this chapter will be useful guidelines for structuring, refining, and expanding the reader's mental models about creating and communicating decision support information.

This discussion might start by identifying the types of questions usually asked of the decision support created in the practice of institutional research. It is clear that to create quality decision support data and information, institutional researchers must have an understanding of the institution, its structure, and its processes. They must also have an understanding of the issues and values that are driving the decision makers to make a decision. Providing a structure for creating useful decision support at all levels of decision making, Colonel Richard Medsger, director of the Office of Institutional Research, West Point, in 1970 asked three questions of his staff when they reported the results of studies they had conducted about the academy. These three questions are sequential in nature, requiring that the first be answered before the second and the second before the third:

1. What did you find?
   To answer this question, the institutional research professional conducting the analysis simply provides a description of the specific data and information that have been produced. The results of the analysis are described without comment about meaning or implications. This level of analysis usually is needed to react to external reporting mandates and requires a technical understanding of the institution's data and data structures and the skills needed to manipulate the data.
2. What does it mean?
   Answering this question requires that the institutional researcher interpret the findings within the context of the institution, its processes, and its structure. Most often this level of analysis supports the management of operational processes (registration, payroll, and so on). Knowledge of the organization and how its processes and structures facilitate the interaction of students, faculty, administrators, and staff are required of the institutional researcher working at this level.
3. So what?
   This question, often the most difficult to answer, asks the institutional researcher to interpret the findings within the context of the

decision-making process. In other words, the institutional researcher must understand the context, both internally and externally, in which the decision maker is to operate. The information must be communicated in a form that is consistent with this environment and outline the potential consequences of various courses of action.

Three Tiers of Intelligence

Terenzini (1993) has identified three tiers of intelligence that provide insights about the knowledge and skills necessary to answer the previous three questions. The first tier, *technical intelligence,* includes methodological skills and the ability to use statistical packages and to conduct studies that would include surveys; cost-benefit analyses; and other data collection, manipulation, and analysis activities. This level of intelligence or skills reflects the abilities needed to meet the day-to-day operations of an institutional research office or function and typically involves the restructuring and analysis of numerical data. The second tier, *issues intelligence,* includes an understanding of the institution's processes, how decisions are made, and how to study complex issues such as student retention or salary equity. Individuals functioning at this level of intelligence have organizational skills, good communication skills, and the ability to use methodologies and knowledge from multiple disciplines to design a study and interpret its results. The third tier, *contextual intelligence,* reflects an understanding of the institutional and general culture of higher education, how business is done at the institution, and how to effect change. Working at this level of intelligence allows the institutional researcher to provide information to the decision maker that provides insights about different alternatives that reflect the values of the decision maker and their potential outcomes. Working at this level of intelligence, the institutional research professional integrates both quantitative and qualitative information in support of decision making.

These models provide institutional researchers with a framework for evaluating the level at which they are working and the potential value of the decision support information to different decision makers across the campus. In general, those offices that focus on meeting accountability mandates are responding to the question "What did you find?" and are functioning with technical intelligence. On the other hand, those that are directly supporting senior leadership across the campus, addressing the "So what?" question, employ contextual intelligence in the creation and interpretation of decision support information.

Levels of Decision Support

Institutional research is involved in the support of three types of activities that occur simultaneously at colleges and universities. McLaughlin and McLaughlin (1989) describe these types of activities as processes that occur across all levels of the institution and that require both continuous and specific one-time information support. *Operational-level processes* are those "mechanisms that run and monitor the transformation of inputs into outputs" (p. 23). These processes tend to be short term and are managed by well-defined and understood rules and policies. In general, these structured processes require little judgment on the part of managers as the work, goals, and resources are guided by specific institutional policies and procedures. Decision support of these processes (for example, registration, class scheduling, maintenance) requires the development of systems that provide, on a continuous or periodic basis, well-defined data and information for monitoring their efficiency (typically quantitative information) and effectiveness (quantitative and qualitative information).

Managerial-level processes are conducted from an institutional perspective and tend to " . . . focus on the allocation and reallocation of resources . . ." (p. 22). These processes tend to deal with issues that have limited time perspectives and most often are concerned with budget allocations or changes within the institution or its external environment. Support of these processes usually requires the analysis of trend data and evaluative information developed on an annual or semi-annual basis. In addition, specific studies (salary studies, retention studies, and so on) are designed to provide information about the impact of changes in policies and processes, the environment, or to gain insights about unexpected behavior or trends that support managerial-level processes. *Strategic-level processes* are activities that "involve the identification, development, and focus of overall organizational efforts" (p. 22). These efforts address issues of longer-range timeframes and typically involve participation from all levels of the institution. These processes at most campuses tend to be episodic in nature and are driven by changes in senior personnel or external mandates (accreditation or legislative review). In these cases, decision support consists of the analysis of input and productivity data and information as well as the results of special studies (for example, institutional impact studies) that address concerns of senior leadership.

Each of these processes requires different types of data and information support. In each case, however, the processes require both formative and summative assessment, that is, asking how the process is working and the adequacy or quality of what it produces. Decision support can, and often will, reflect both quantitative and qualitative data and information for each of these processes.

The Decision-Making Process

Decisions of varying magnitude are made daily in our institutions. Many of these decisions are made at the operational level and have minimal impact on the overall direction or health of the institution, its faculty, its staff, and its administrators and occur as a part of normal institutional activities. However, at senior leadership and managerial levels, decisions are often made after a good deal of thought and study. Decision making may be thought of as a sequential set of activities on the part of the decision maker. Cyert, Simon, and Trow (1983) have defined a sequential seven-step process that identifies specific activities at each point in the decision-making process. An understanding of where the decision maker is in this process will provide insights about the nature and structure of the needed support. At some points in the process, the desired or needed support may require the collection and analysis of qualitative data. In other cases, information generated from the analysis of quantitative data may be necessary. Obviously, in all cases, both forms of decision support may be necessary. The following are the seven sequential steps:

1. Identify the problem leading to a need to make a decision.
2. Clarify the issues related to the situation and focus on the problem.
3. Identify feasible alternatives, one of which is to avoid making a decision at this time.
4. Select the criteria for selecting the preferred alternatives.
5. Support the decision that has been made and lobby for support of the position taken.
6. Induce action in others to implement change.
7. Measure and evaluate outcomes associated with the desired change.

The manager or administrator may be seeking assistance in one or all of these steps. In fact, support may be needed at several points in the sequence, and multiple analyses and projects might be requested. In any case, it is important to establish timelines for completing the project and developing an understanding about what is to be learned and how it will support the decision-making process. This final clarification should provide an understanding of the context in which the decision is to be made and provide the institutional researcher with insights about the most effective manner of communicating the results of the project.

Characteristics of Decision-Making Philosophies

Decision makers use various decision-making philosophies in their management of the institution. It is important that the institutional researcher understand the philosophy that is being supported, as each one demands that the support reflect specific attributes if it is to be effective. In Table 3.1, four decision-making philosophies are presented along with the decision maker's primary context of concern and information requirements (adapted from McLaughlin, McLaughlin, and Howard, 1987).

In the *political decision-making philosophy*, others' perceptions are of primary concern. Usually key executives dealing with external and internal constituents use this. As these individuals are typically busy, the most

Table 3.1. Characteristics of Decision-Making Philosophies

Decision-Making Philosophy	Context Primary Concern	Information Requirements Focus	Breadth
Political	Others' perceptions	Discrete	Focused
Autocratic	Personal agenda	Continuous	Focused
Managerial	Program quality	Continuous	Broad
Collegial	Correctness of process	Discrete	Broad

effective information support is often in the form of discrete bits of information focused on a specific topic or concern. This might be a single enrollment figure or the average salary of full professors. Generally, the desirability of specific outcomes and the causes of these outcomes are of lesser value to these decision makers. Typically, decisions are based on a complex set of relationships and influences that are often political and or situational.

In the *autocratic decision-making philosophy,* the decision maker's personal agenda relative to an organization such as a college or major research center is the primary focus. The decision maker often prefers a continuous flow of information as it relates to his or her agenda but often likes to have it delivered in focused bits. There is less concern about the desirability of different outcomes because preferences are focused on personal agendas. There is, however, usually an interest in the best or most efficient process that will result in a specific outcome.

The *managerial decision-making philosophy* occurs where there are a large number of issues. In these situations, unstructured decision-making processes are often required. There is the need for persuasive arguments by the manager and a participatory decision process. The primary concern is for program quality where both effectiveness and efficiency are important such as in an academic department or program. In general, these decision makers are interested in a broad and continuous flow of data and information that describes the quality (productivity and outcomes) of their programs. They often use a rational decision model and greatly value the types of information that institutional research can provide. They are interested in the causation of desired outcomes.

Finally, the *collegial decision-making philosophy* is present on virtually every campus. Here the primary concern is correctness of process. In supporting this type of decision making, the institutional researcher needs to provide discrete bits of information or data covering broadly the issues under consideration. Virtually every aspect of the situation that the decision maker thinks might be relevant will be examined. Great care is often taken to ensure that all perspectives are considered. Often, the initial discussions focus on the desirability of various outcomes and less on the causation of the outcomes.

Uses of Information

Ewell (1989) has presented five primary ways that administrators and institutional leaders use information. Understanding the way in which a decision maker intends to use the information that an institutional researcher creates often provides guidelines for the type of information needed and how to present it to the decision maker.

Identify Problems. In this case, the information is used to inform the campus or specific constituencies that a problem exists. The information may come in the form of descriptive information that compares targets with actual performance or productivity. Quantitative information should reflect a few key indicators and be presented in a way that highlights the differences. Identifying a problem requires simplicity in the presentation of data or information (quantitative or qualitative) and can be made more effective by the use of graphics.

Setting the Context for a Decision. The purpose of using the information in this type of situation is to provide a context within which a decision is to be made. The intent is to create a holistic picture of the institutional processes and culture that will be impacted by or will itself impact the decision. Information best suited for this type of support includes qualitative information generated from discussions internally and externally combined with the quantitative information that documents the situation.

Rational Decision Making. In a classical sense, this activity involves the identification and analysis of alternative courses of action. The intent is to reduce the uncertainty associated with the decision by examining potential outcomes of different courses of action. The focus of these analyses is typically on identifying alternatives with the greatest potential for benefit while incurring the least cost. If the decision maker is rational, information from these analyses will be quite useful and impact the decision regardless of the form in which it is supplied.

Inducing Action. In these situations, the intent of this type of supporting information is to reduce uncertainty resulting in a decision being made. The key issue in these types of situations is to reduce conflict created by differences in values or desired outcomes. This is particularly relevant when multiple parties are involved in the decision-making process and bring their own contextual perspective to the discussion. Providing concrete data about the problem for all constituencies to study may be as important as its informational content in bringing closure to the discussion and a decision being made.

Promoting or Legitimizing a Decision. At this point, a decision has been made, and the need is for information that promotes the rationality of the decision and actions to be taken. Effective support in these types of situations typically takes the form of quantitatively based descriptive information. Complex data collection methodologies and statistical analyses may result in competing parties not understanding, and as such, not believing the results or buying into the decision.

Another View of Rational Decision Making

Rational decision support as previously described reflects an analytical process in which models are built that reflect various alternatives that a decision maker can make and their potential outcomes. In general, these analyses are quantitative in nature and revolve around the relationships of needed resources and outcomes. While these models provide important information, their usefulness in the decision making process should be viewed as a starting point. In Figure 3.1, a process of rational decision making is presented that reflects the creation of information (quantitative or qualitative) that is integrated into the knowledge base of the decision makers and other constituencies across the campus. The result of this integration is the creation of intelligence that is then brought to bear on the decision that needs to be made. In this process, the empirical information is analyzed, interpreted, and integrated into the knowledge base of the decision makers. The resulting intelligence comprises both the results of the data analysis and the decision maker's existing knowledge about the context in which the decision is to be made. Once a decision is made, assessment of the impact of the decision provides the campus with increased organizational intelligence and the process of rational decision making begins again. Critical in this process is the ability to access valid and reliable data and, through appropriate analyses, create quality information and communicate effectively its meaning to decision makers.

Creating Quality Decision Support

Key to any form of decision support is the creation of quality data and information. In this case, quality data accurately reflects the construct or issue that is being studied, and quality information is defined as information that is useful in the decision-making process. During the past decade, Gerry McLaughlin and I have developed and written about a conceptual model that describes a process for the creation of quality decision support information. Presented in Figure 3.2, this model reflects five sequential steps and three roles. The detailed description of these steps and the roles can be found in McLaughlin, Howard, Balkan, and Blythe (1998).

My intent in presenting this model is to reinforce the notion that the creation of quality decision support information is a sequential process that requires input and cooperation from those individuals responsible for

1. The initial collection and storage of the data.
2. The use of the resulting information to make decisions.
3. The producer of the information who must communicate it in a way that is useful to the decision maker.

This final role is typically that of the institutional research professional. As described previously, the role requires skills needed to access and ana-

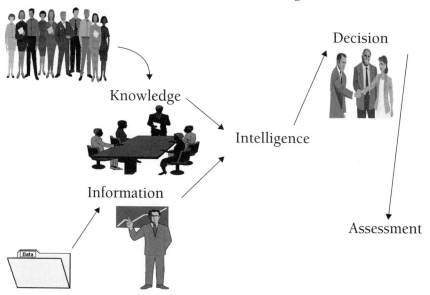

Figure 3.1. Rational Decision-Making Process

Decision

Knowledge

Intelligence

Information

Assessment

Data

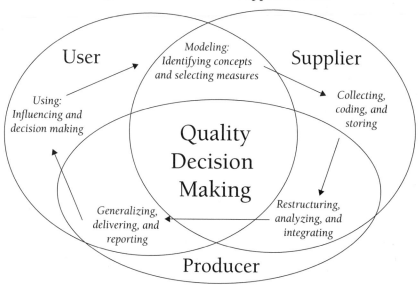

Figure 3.2. Information Support Process

User

Supplier

Modeling:
Identifying concepts
and selecting measures

Using:
Influencing and
decision making

Collecting,
coding, and
storing

Quality
Decision
Making

Generalizing,
delivering, and
reporting

Restructuring,
analyzing, and
integrating

Producer

lyze data, communication skills that will provide the decision maker with an understanding of what the results of the analysis mean, and finally the ability to provide the decision maker with information that directly relates to the decision that has to be made. Note that this process is circular in nature, indicating that quality decision support is an ongoing activity that requires an assessment of the usefulness of the information in the decision-making process. With this information, the institutional researcher can both evaluate the quality of the decision support provided and identify potential measures to be used to evaluate the outcomes of the decision.

Conclusions

Remember that sometimes an administrator or manager is faced with a difficult choice or decision (for example, whether to lay off individuals or eliminate programs). The decision often will be put off for as long as possible. In general, the decision makers will indicate that they just do not have enough data to make the decision. When it finally becomes impossible to delay any more, the decision will be made, and blame for any hardship will be directed at the data: "The data are conclusive and gave me no other choice." These situations will occur regardless of the quality of the information one may provide.

Situations like that will occur, and the behavior of the administrator cannot be controlled by the institutional research professional. However, quality decision support (and hopefully more informed decisions) can be provided when communicated within the context of the institution and the information needs of the decision maker.

The intent of this chapter is to provide basic frameworks within which institutional researchers can structure decision support at their institutions. The conceptual models presented reflect processes and components of different aspects of decision support. These conceptual models can be used as a starting point for individuals developing their own mental models to help them navigate through their institutions.

References

Cyert, R. M., Simon, H. M., and Trow, D. B. "Observation of a Business Decision." In Herbert A. Simon (ed.), *Models of Bounded Rationality,* Vol. 2: *Behavioral Economics and Business Organization.* Cambridge, Mass.: MIT Press, 1983.

Ewell, P. T. "Information for Decision: What's the Use?" In P. T. Ewell (ed.), *Enhancing Information Use in Decision Making.* New Directions for Institutional Research, no. 64. San Francisco: Jossey-Bass, 1989.

McLaughlin, G. W., Howard, R. D., Balkan, L. A., and Blythe, E. W. *People, Processes and Data Administration.* Resources in Institutional Research, no. 11. Tallahassee, Fla.: Association for Institutional Research, 1998.

McLaughlin, G. W., and McLaughlin, J. S. "Barriers to Information Use: The Organizational Context." In P. T. Ewell (ed.), *Enhancing Information Use in Decision Making.* New Directions for Institutional Research, no. 64. San Francisco: Jossey-Bass, 1989.

McLaughlin, G. W., McLaughlin, J. S., and Howard, R. D. "Decision Support in the Information Age." In E. M. Staman (ed.), *Managing Information in Higher Education.* New Directions for Institutional Research, no. 55. San Francisco: Jossey-Bass, 1987.

Senge, P. M. *The Fifth Discipline: The Art and Practice of the Learning Organization.* New York: Currency Doubleday, 1990.

Senge, P. M., and others. *The Fifth Discipline Fieldbook.* New York: Currency Doubleday, 1994.

Terenzini, P. T. "On the Nature of Institutional Research and the Knowledge and Skills It Requires." *The Journal of Research in Higher Education, 34*(1), 1–10.

RICHARD D. HOWARD *is associate professor of adult and higher education at Montana State University–Bozeman.*

4

Providing appropriate contextual information when reporting quantitative information is a necessary role that will not be replaced or subsumed by technological advances in data and information retrieval systems.

Communicating Qualitative and Quantitative Decision Support Information

Marsha K. Moss

Institutional research offices spend substantial time and resources collecting, cleansing, manipulating, analyzing, and reporting data to various constituent groups. However, the basic function of institutional research is transforming data into information to support planning and decision making (Saupe, 1981). To that end, not only must information be timely, accurate, and relevant, but to be useful to the decision maker, it must also be presented in the proper context. By *context,* I mean weaving into the data-based information additional information to give it coherence and completeness, relating the information to the issues that are confronting the decision maker. This contextual placement increases the value of and confidence in the information, making it more likely to be used in the decision process.

Over time, my communication of qualitative and quantitative information has evolved. I have served as the director of an institutional research office at a major research institution for almost twenty years; however, my first position in higher education was as a computer programmer. With degrees in statistics and management information systems, my first concern was with the quality, consistency, accuracy, and reliability of the data collected, maintained, and ultimately used by decision makers on campus. Designing files and systems for effective and efficient data capture and retrieval was my primary focus. With additional experience in the organization, I began to develop a sense of how the institution operated and what the major policy issues were, at least the ones about which the institutional research office was providing data and information. In Terenzini's terms (1993), I came to the institution with technical/analytical intelligence and began developing issues intelligence. Strong technical and analytical skills, along with decent writing and verbal communication skills, were instrumental in my appointment as director of the institutional research office some years later. As Terenzini (1993) stresses, these technical/analytical skills are necessary but not sufficient in providing effective decision support, a fact of which I was blissfully ignorant at the start of my career.

My development as an institutional research professional paralleled the development of our institutional research office. The focus in the 1970s was on developing good, reliable data systems and sources from which management information could be generated. The reputation and credibility of the office, within and outside the institution, were built on the high-quality information and analytical services it provided.

My communication focused principally on presenting quantitative information and analyses as clearly, logically, and concisely as possible. The goal of the communication was to ensure that the decision maker had confidence in the information and understood what it meant so that he or she could consider it in the decision process. The format tended to be brief and more formal, with discussion focusing on how the information was compiled and how reliable it was. Presentations to external audiences might have also included some explanation of the issues confronting the institution or the arena in which it operated. Internally, this type of information was alluded to only briefly. After all, the executives understood the issues much better than I did.

Although the services and communications mentioned previously are necessary in providing decision support, they are not sufficient. In Chapter Six of this volume, Mark Perkins asserts that institutional research professionals are most helpful to decision makers when they "build a broad context for institutional decision making grounded in quantitative and qualitative inputs from multiple perspectives." He goes on to describe how the president must interact and communicate with the institutional research professional so that he or she can provide the level of support the decision maker needs.

The institutional research professional must also take the initiative and responsibility for ensuring that dialogue with decision makers is occurring. Developing knowledge of the culture of your institution and of higher education in general (or contextual intelligence, as Terenzini [1993] refers to it) and using that knowledge in routine and ad hoc decision support activities may be the only way to initiate this dialogue.

From my own experience, I have found that this type of intelligence has allowed me to change my communication style and the interactions that I have with decision makers. Although I am still asked to present data and information to answer specific questions, I am also part of the executive team, especially in the provost's office, which discusses the issues, prepares and compares alternatives, and makes decisions and action plans to carry out those decisions. My office and I have additional credibility because we are able to tailor the quantitative and qualitative data and information we assemble into a context specifically suited to our institution.

Generally, the communication format is informal and conversational and can range from sixty-second encounters in the hall or lounge to day-long planning retreats. A brief exchange in the hall with the provost or president might focus on the composition of an advisory committee on funding formulas appointed by the state coordinating council. My recommendation might be that the executive attend some of their meetings to present the views of a major research institution or ask that such a representative be appointed to the committee.

Typically, qualitative issues receive more discussion time than quantitative information presentations and very often focus on the political and financial implications of different courses of action. During a daylong planning retreat, the session usually begins with a relatively brief presentation of a good amount of quantitative information to identify issues and set the stage for discussion. The discussion is usually quite lengthy, with participants giving the perspectives of the constituent groups they represent, their views of appropriate actions and of political and often financial obstacles, and the ramifications of different courses of action. As recommendations are formed, participants usually come back to the quantitative data presented earlier to support those recommendations. To be an effective participant in these planning processes, the institutional research professional must be able to contribute to the contextual, qualitative discussions.

The following questions are among those that I routinely ask myself when trying to develop the context in which to disseminate information:

- What do I know about the decision makers' views on the topic?
- What are their prejudices and biases on this issue?
- What language do they use in describing the issue?
- What material have they seen in the past, and is it consistent with my information?
- What previous policy decisions have they or their predecessors made in this area and why?
- What would it take to change their position on an issue?
- Which constituents will be affected by the decision and how?
- What are the political implications or costs among alternative decisions, and how can these costs be compared or minimized?
- What are the financial implications of this decision?
- How do my findings relate to national, regional, or state initiatives or other studies?
- What policy decisions have peer departments, institutions, or states made regarding the issue?

Context Is Qualitative

The context the institutional research professional provides is, in many cases, the qualitative factor in the information dissemination process. Researchers, by virtue of the fact that they live at the institution, perform qualitative research on a daily basis. They bring perspectives from observations and from their own experiences in the organization. They know "the reality of the situation by being there, by becoming immersed in the stream of events and activities, by becoming part of the phenomenon of study, and by documenting the understanding of the situation by those engaged in it" (Hathaway, 1999, p. 279). They have an insider's perspective and also solicit others' perceptions through formal and informal interviews or contacts (Fetterman, 1991). To be most effective in setting the broader context, researchers "must attend to the total situation and integrate information from all directions simultaneously" (Hathaway, 1999, p. 280), including other experience in higher education settings gained from networking, studying, and observing.

Terenzini (1993) terms this *contextual intelligence,* or the form of organizational intelligence "that earns institutional research and researchers legitimacy, trust, and respect" (pp. 5–6). He further defines it as knowledge about higher education in general and the specifics about one's own institution and its culture. This includes a broad familiarity with all aspects of the enterprise, from its history, philosophy, mission, internal and external governance, and politics to its traditions, management styles, and constituents served. It is knowledge about the environment in which our institutions operate and what opportunities and constraints are encountered within it. Terenzini (1993) goes on to assert that contextual intelligence is acquired through on-the-job training and provides a list of activities that institutional researchers must engage in to acquire this knowledge.

Communication

The art of communicating is relating to individuals, listening to them and understanding what their motivations and orientations are, finding common interests and experiences, and establishing rapport with others by relating our beliefs and experiences to theirs. This results in an exchange of thoughts and ideas between the parties involved that hopefully leads to greater understanding. The institutional researcher must follow this same process when communicating information. By establishing linkages to the decision maker's agendas and incorporating their terminology, or at least establishing linkages to their terminology, the recipient will be better able to understand and relate to the information. Conveying an understanding of the implications of the decision from policy, political, or financial perspectives lends credibility both to the presenter and the information being presented. Offering alternatives, with an assessment of the positive and negative implications of various scenarios, provides additional context in the decision support process.

To be effective, institutional researchers must not only be able to convey or transmit their message but must also be active listeners who are able to determine what is needed and not just what is being requested. Determining needed information is often a more complicated process.

Because of the demands placed on the leaders of our institutions, it is not always possible to communicate with them directly or in person. Often requests for information from presidents, provosts, and other executive officers are received via e-mail or from an assistant or other third party. It can be difficult to ask follow-up questions and determine the purpose and the intended audience for the request in these situations. Knowing the current issues facing leaders by knowing the institutional environment can help, but following up with a clarifying e-mail message and, if necessary, asking for some insight from the assistant or other individuals who might have attended the meeting where the request originated is a good practice. In some cases it may be necessary to ask for a ten-minute, face-to-face meeting to clarify the request.

Good Practices Regarding Quantitative Information

Although there are always exceptions to any rule, the following illustrate some good practices for disseminating quantitative information, which includes information generated from surveys or other statistical analyses:

1. Reformatting computer output often makes the information more easily understood and adds value to the information. This would include summarizing, creating totals or ratios, or changing the data's orientation (See Bers and Seybert, 1999, for presentation recommendations).

2. Provide a brief narrative analysis of the information along with the detail in tables and graphs to add context to the information. Even if the information has been presented before and the table is an update with the most recent year's data, describing the changes from the previous year or from five years ago will assist the decision maker in using the material.

3. Whenever possible, use official census data that are consistent with reports to external agencies. The official fall enrollment total reported on the Integrated Postsecondary Education Data System Fall Enrollment Survey should agree with what is reported to the trustees and the state coordinating council and used in the institution's factbook and other internal reports.

4. Prepare brief (one to two pages), regular analyses on issues of importance to the campus and leaders in time to be used routinely in the decision-making process. These analyses should incorporate short tables or graphs, with more detailed tables and descriptions of statistical methods included as appendixes. Enrollment analyses, retention and graduation studies, faculty and administrator salary and fringe benefit comparisons, expenditures comparisons, and other benchmarks with peer institutions can be effectively utilized in ongoing decision processes.

5. When analyzing data, monitor for exceptions and anomalies and convey significant findings to institution executives. For example, a recent policy change on the classification of entering graduate students would have negatively affected our institution's formula-driven state appropriation. By

noticing this change early and realizing the funding implications, information was gathered and presented by the institutional research office to those initiating the policy change (and to other executive staff), and the policy was reversed before it affected the University of Texas at Austin's funding level significantly.

6. Be aware of important initiatives that have been undertaken at the institution and make sure data systems are in place or are being developed to monitor those initiatives. For example, in Texas, a recent law guarantees all students in the top 10 percent of their high school graduating class admission to any public institution. The calculation of this ranking is very specific, and our institution has funded new scholarship programs to attract top 10 percent students from targeted high schools across the state. The student-tracking system used in retention and graduation analyses has been modified to capture this new high school rank calculation and to identify the special scholarship recipients so that these new initiatives can be monitored for effectiveness over time.

Good Practices Regarding Qualitative Information

Qualitative information, or the information gathered by observation, interviews, or focus groups, must also be presented concisely to be effectively used in the decision process. Bers and Seybert (1999) offer several options for reporting information from focus group research and warn against presenting findings in numerical tables and summaries. However, a full narrative report that might include all comments pertaining to a specific question or idea is not one a busy executive is likely to take the time to read. Instead, identifying major categories into which most of the observations fit and illustrating the categories with selected quotations from the focus group participants can be quite effective. Providing interpretations of the findings and recommendations, in the context of the issues facing the institution, also increases the effectiveness of the qualitative information being presented.

Presentation Considerations

Through personal interactions with the decision maker—whether it's one-on-one, in a meeting, or listening to her address the faculty, trustees, students, or legislative leadership—the institutional researcher can learn her communication, analytical, and decision-making styles. This understanding is essential so that information be formatted and presented in a manner that the executive can easily understand, assimilate, and use. Often, the decision maker's academic discipline will signal how best to present information and the extent to which he or she usually relies on information in policy decisions. Some individuals prefer narrative, with tables or appendices as backup material. Some leaders are visual and prefer information to be presented graphically; others prefer tables and lists with brief narrative descriptions and analyses, and some would be just as happy analyzing the information themselves. In the latter case, it is even more important for the institutional researcher to put the information in context by providing brief interpretations and describing data limitations and appropriate uses. (In this situation, I would recommend that this be done very subtly, of course.)

In *Effective Reporting,* an excellent resource on presenting qualitative and quantitative information, Bers and Seybert (1999) describe the reporting process and the types of reports that are most effective with different audiences. Presidents and other executives "learn from simple charts and plain language; need information on key, often quantitative, indicators . . . read selectively . . . and expect conclusions, implications, and recommendations to be expressed clearly" (p. 8). This view was confirmed by Richard Yanikoski (2000), president of St. Xavier University, when he addressed the National Postsecondary Education Cooperative Council recently. Yanikoski's central premise was that "complex issues and crowded days negatively impact the president's ability to make sound decisions swiftly and precisely" and to make adequate use of data in decision making. He further asserted that most presidents use much less information than they receive and usually use data to justify decisions they have already made.

Timeliness and Timing. Allowing sufficient lead time for the decision maker to receive, digest, and incorporate the information in his or her decision making process is fundamental. Sufficient time is required to incorporate information into presentations to internal audiences (faculty committees and trustees) as well as external audiences (legislators and editorial boards).

Again, because the decision maker usually receives more information than can possibly be used, it is important to time the dissemination of the information appropriately and suggest how and when it will be useful. At most of our institutions, there is a regular schedule of events year after year. The trustees meet every quarter; the legislature, every spring; and budget hearings are every fall. By being aware of the issues that the president wants to promote or with which legislators are concerned, supporting material can be prepared and presented to the president and other executives several weeks before scheduled hearings or meetings. The report or analysis will be current, more easily remembered, and more likely to be used.

For example, every September, there are budget hearings at which our president makes a presentation to the Legislative Budget Board, appropriation committee staff, and representatives from the governor's office. Knowing that one of the issues to be discussed at these hearings is performance measures, a packet of material dealing with them is always prepared and provided to him several weeks before the first hearing. Also, knowing that one of the president's legislative initiatives for this session is a flexible tuition plan, comparative tuition and fee information and other tuition analyses were also resubmitted to him in time to incorporate the information in his presentation. Even though the president had received most of this information months before, it was important to send it to him again with additional contextual information for ease of use.

Clarity and Integrity. Not only must the information be accurate, relevant, and consistent, but it should also, according to President Yanikoski, have definitional clarity. As a standard practice, all tables, graphs, and figures should contain basic information. Typically, the institution name, the office preparing the report, the date, sources used, explanatory notes, and any cautionary statements about the sources or uses of the data should be on the table, even if they are included in the narrative of the report. Once the information leaves the institutional research office, there is no way of ensuring that graphs and tables will not be copied and distributed without the explanatory narrative.

Brevity and Portability. Remembering the time constraints under which our decision makers operate, it is important that the information provided be easily accessible, concise, and portable. Information that can be reviewed on the airplane, in the hotel room, or in the van on the way to a presentation is more likely to be used. This reinforces the idea that the communication of decision support information should be clear and succinct. The detail can be appended to the report or document. President Yanikoski stresses that "the practical significance must exceed the statistical significance" of the information.

Audience. Bers and Seybert (1999) challenge institutional research professionals to tailor communication of information to each audience. Orienting the presentation style and material to the intended audience is important in the visual sense and critical in the contextual sense.

For example, information from a survey of freshmen who were retained or left the institution after one year may be presented to institutional research professionals, executives, faculty policy committees, and student affairs personnel and advisers. The same summary or statistical tables can be used for these different audiences when time will not allow for tailoring. However, the qualitative or narrative description of these tables and their meaning can be described in terms that relate the information or data to the individuals' different orientations, perspectives, and agendas, providing unique decision support to each of the various groups.

How to Prepare

After understanding why the information is being requested, what decision it is intended to inform, whose opinion it is intended to influence, and how to compile the quantitative or qualitative material, the institutional researcher must determine the context in which to present or communicate the information to the intended audience. How does one capture the attention of the user, relate the information to the user's interests and agendas in his or her own language, and convince the user that the material prepared should be considered in the decision-making process?

The first step is reviewing what is known about the individual or group receiving the information. This phase of preparation is analogous to using a Web search engine to find sites pertaining to a topic. The researcher must scan his or her memory banks and other storage devices for all relevant sites regarding the intended user or audience. For those of us suffering from information overload or who have had our directories corrupted and information is no longer easily retrievable, organizations' (including our institutions) Web sites contain a wealth of information. In addition to quantitative data for which institutional research professionals routinely search, policies and regulations, legislation, planning documents, mission statements, studies and publications, organization charts, news releases, and even addresses and speeches are often available on-line to help one learn about the audience.

Next comes the filtering process. One by one, each tangential link must be examined to determine if the site contains information that is relevant to this specific presentation. Fortunately, in the previous step, our memory banks can usually perform sophisticated searches joining two or more key words, so the number of sites to investigate is manageable.

After the relevant set of questions has been answered, the researcher can prepare the contextual data set that will accompany his or her other information. The amount of contextual information presented may vary depending on whether the presentation is formal or informal. Generally in a formal setting, the contextual information is used to briefly introduce or preface the quantitative and other qualitative findings, may be sprinkled in as the findings are being presented, and may be cited extensively in the question-and-answer segment. In an informal setting or meeting, contextual information may become the central focus of the discussion and be relied on more heavily in the decision process. However, once consensus is reached in the discussion phase, quantitative data invariably are used to justify the decisions.

Conclusion

To provide the most effective decision support to our leaders, institutional research professionals must possess technical/analytical intelligence, issues intelligence, and contextual intelligence (Terenzini, 1993). Although the first two types of intelligence are necessary to establish credibility within our institutions, they are not sufficient for complete decision support. The institutional research professional must have contextual intelligence, or the knowledge of the culture of the institution, and provide this context with whatever type of information is being communicated to executives. This essential role of the institutional research professional, a provider of context, is one that cannot and will not be subsumed by technological advances in data and information retrieval systems on our campuses. The communication component of the institutional research function as described here is one that must be mastered by the institutional research professional. If not, the role of the institutional research professional will often revolve around the technical aspects of collecting and analyzing data, not on supporting the full information needs of the institution's senior decision makers.

References

Bers, T. H., and Seybert, J. A. *Effective Reporting.* Tallahassee, Fla.: Association for Institutional Research, 1999.

Fetterman, D. M. "Editor's Notes." In D. M. Fetterman (ed.), *Using Qualitative Methods in Institutional Research.* New Directions for Institutional Research, no. 72. San Francisco: Jossey-Bass, 1991.

Hathaway, R. S. "Assumptions Underlying Quantitative and Qualitative Research: Implications for Institutional Research." In M. W. Peterson (ed.), *ASHE Reader on Planning and Institutional Research.* Needham Heights, Mass.: Pearson, 1999.

Saupe, J. L. *The Functions of Institutional Research.* Tallahassee, Fla.: Association for Institutional Research, 1981.

Terenzini, P. T. "On the Nature of Institutional Research and the Knowledge and Skills It Requires." *Research in Higher Education,* 1993, *34*(1), 1–10.

Yanikoski, R. "From Better Decisions to Better Data: A President's View." Speech presented at the 6th Annual National Postsecondary Education Cooperative Council Meeting, Washington, D.C., November 30, 2000.

MARSHA K. MOSS is assistant vice president and director of institutional studies at the University of Texas at Austin.

5

It is important to bring both quantitative and qualitative information to bear on critical academic decisions in order to supplant perceptions and anecdotal data that often undermine confidence and morale in the academy.

Using Qualitative and Quantitative Information in Academic Decision Making

Ann S. Ferren, Martin S. Aylesworth

Academic affairs administrators have long relied on institutional researchers for information and research in a variety of areas to support planning and decision making. Increasingly, the demands on the institutional research office, the variety of users of information, and the complexity of issues to be managed necessitate a clearer understanding of how academic administrators, faculty, and institutional researchers can work together to improve the information necessary for effective planning and decision making. Equally important is the need to bring both quantitative and qualitative research to bear on critical academic decisions to provide a better context for information and to supplant perceptions and anecdotal data that so often undermine confidence and morale in the academy.

Enhancing the Relationship Between Institutional Research and Academic Affairs

Traditionally, the institutional research office is seen as the source and center of control of all academic information. Faculty call for quick answers to questions such as the average salary for associate professors so that they can make a case for a salary increase. The president calls for the number of living alumni to be put into a speech. Admissions counselors call for the student-faculty ratio to reassure parents when recruiting prospective students. In an effort to make such snapshot institutional data more readily available, institutional research offices produce factbooks. With factbooks now available electronically, deans, department chairs, and faculty can find relevant information for their planning and decision making and descriptive data for their reports and speeches. Too often, however, the bits of information, point-in-time measures, or simple comparisons are misleading as the institutional research office necessarily provides little interpretation or context for their use. This allows users to bring their own perspectives and biases to the interpretation of the data.

It is not uncommon for faculty committees or department chairs, who can now easily access the data, to prepare persuasive reports stating "Our classes are too large," "Our students aren't very good," and "Our salaries are too low." Once such faculty perceptions are reinforced by these data, even though the perceptions are based on a limited understanding of how to interpret the available information, the perceptions are very difficult to change. Unfortunately, institutional research offices do not have the time or staff to help these would-be researchers develop the skills necessary to appropriately interpret the information of interest to them.

Consequently, although they are usually strong proponents of open information, many academic affairs administrators, especially deans and vice presidents, regretfully find themselves challenging conclusions and trying to explain that the selected information does not really mean what the user thinks it does. Through several examples, this chapter will suggest ways to establish meaningful contexts for the interpretation of academic information. Further, it will describe how to involve faculty and other administrators in the analysis and interpretation of data and in the subsequent decision-making process to reduce the potential for an adversarial relationship and increase confidence in the results.

In Chapter Three of this issue, Richard Howard describes the decision-making process using a model defined by Cyert, Simon, and Trow (1983) and describes ways that decision makers use information, using a model outlined by Ewell (1989). Two common elements in both of these are promoting a decision and inducing action. That is to say, promoting a decision and inducing action are both essential parts of the decision-making process and are also common examples of ways that decision makers use information. We suggest that these can be combined by involving those who are affected by decisions—those to whom one must promote the decision and those who must be induced to action—by including representatives of these groups in the planning, collection, and analysis of data affecting such decisions. It is, for example, far easier and more effective to get faculty to support a decision and to contribute to its implementation if they have been a part of the planning, data collection, and analysis process than it is to try to persuade and induce them based on results presented by institutional researchers or administrators without having involved them in the process.

In addition to the need for more collaborative processes in academic decision making, there is also a need for more intense, complex institutional research to respond to the increasingly difficult decisions that academic affairs administrators must make. Where once the administrator could rely on descriptive data, trend analyses, and comparative studies to understand an issue or situation, a variety of external pressures, including limited resources, public skepticism, and legislative accountability, now require academic administrators to be able to meet new standards of quality and efficiency. The responsive academic affairs administrator must answer questions such as these: How can the curriculum be more efficient? What changes in hiring practices will overcome the difficulty of hiring in certain fields? What factors are contributing to low faculty morale? How can we increase the graduation rate of first-generation students? To fully understand these issues and the consequences of alternative choices requires both qualitative and quantitative approaches as well as better training of academic administrators in how to use institutional research.

Not only are academic affairs administrators facing more vexing decisions, but they also experience increased pressure for better information faster. The many stakeholders quickly become skeptical and untrusting if they do not get their questions answered immediately. Faculty, who readily question administrative allocation of resources, suspect the worst if they are told the matter is too complex or that they will need to wait months for the data to be analyzed by limited staff. Boards of visitors, made up of business leaders who work by a different calendar than academics, become tentative in their support if they do not have access to hard data on demand. Adding to the challenge of good communication and trust between stakeholders and the administration is the fact that higher education increasingly must be managed with limited resources—indeed, often reduced resources—and the choices among alternative scenarios are value laden. Any vice president for academic affairs committed to continuously improving the institution with these significant constraints must make assessment, evaluation, and institutional research all a high priority, anticipate the kinds of decisions to be made, and be a knowledgeable partner with institutional researchers in the design of appropriate and timely studies.

Examples of Academic Affairs Decision Making

In this section, examples are presented of decisions made in academic affairs that require the support of an integrated and balanced array of qualitative and quantitative information. The examples provided cover three broad areas—decisions related to faculty, decisions related to curricular productivity, and decisions related to student outcomes. For each of the examples, we describe the decision to be made, the relevant contextual factors affecting the decision, the relevant information needed, how the data can be collected, and how the information can be used in making the decision. Both quantitative and qualitative information used in the decision-making process are explained and the processes that engage those affected by the decisions are discussed.

Making Critical Faculty Decisions. Nothing is more important to the quality of an institution than the selection, retention, and evaluation of faculty.

Four issues—the allocation of faculty positions, compensation, workload, and evaluation—provide good examples to describe the points laid out in the previous section.

Authorizing Faculty Positions. Authorizing faculty positions has long appeared to be a political process, with the most persuasive department chair or dean bringing home the bacon. At a minimum, it was expected that each retirement would be replaced within that same department and that any extra positions were up for grabs. Under those assumptions, reversion of all positions to the vice president for academic affairs for potential reallocation or a reduction in the total number of positions is anathema to faculty. Nonetheless, to reshape an institution to meet new demands requires reallocating faculty positions. Without persuasive data on need, the vice president's decision will appear arbitrary and unfair.

To make faculty position allocation a rational process requires careful position control records, a historical record of each faculty position and total full-time equivalent by department, the student credit-hour production over time, the number of majors, trends in the job market for both students and faculty, the optimal class size related to learning outcomes, accreditation requirements, the availability of alternative teaching resources such as part-time and temporary faculty, and the total personnel dollars available. Much of that data is readily available and quantifiable. Far less likely to be available is information on what teaching resources are required to produce particular learning outcomes or student demand for new areas of study such as Asian history or Web design. Consultation with department chairs and faculty is necessary to gather this information.

Unfortunately, few faculty have a perspective of the entire institution and know only about their own unit. To engage faculty and department chairs in understanding how important it is to weigh competing individual interests, to understand that market factors differ by discipline, to recognize that pedagogy is both discipline specific and faculty specific, and to optimize resources, we put together a task force to review the problem of both college-wide and institution-wide faculty position allocation. Members of the task force interviewed department chairs, reviewed career data, and talked with deans about hiring. After considerable study and agreement on fundamental principles, the task force created a report for academic affairs indicating the priorities for decision making, including evidence of student demand, the need for faculty with essential specializations within the existing program, current overreliance on temporary faculty, opportunities for program growth, and the need for additional faculty to enhance the quality and continuity of an existing program.

That report was then widely disseminated to department chairs and faculty and guides their faculty position planning. Although not perfectly understood, some departments now know they are unlikely to keep the position when a colleague retires, others know they are slated for additions each year because of student demand, still other departments readily trade in a French position for a Spanish position or a poet for a technical writer, while yet another unit opts for larger classes to stretch their full-time faculty resources further to meet accreditation standards. By asking faculty and department chairs about the context in which the number of faculty positions is to be understood for their unit, they ask for fewer positions, make better use of them, and have more realistic expectations.

Determining Appropriate Compensation. Faculty compensation—including initial salaries and salary increases—represents one of the most important sets of decisions in higher education, affecting both the institution's ability to recruit and retain quality faculty and its ability to foster good morale among continuing faculty. Few decisions in academic affairs are more closely examined or more frequently questioned than these. However, particularly at a time when budgets are becoming more strained, when competition for faculty in many fields is becoming more intense, and when the disparity between salaries across different disciplines is becoming more pronounced, these decisions are difficult. As a result, the information needed for such decisions must not only be highly reliable and defensible but must also include a wide variety of factors that often require qualitative as well as quantitative data.

For decisions related to authorizing initial salaries of new faculty hires, a variety of quantitative information is pertinent and available. These would include data on previous year new hire salaries offered by peer group institutions (available to members of the College and University Professional Association [CUPA]), data on current salaries by discipline and rank within one's own institution, and additional data on new-hire salaries in specialized programs at one's own institution that may not be comparable to those at peer-group institutions (such as those programs with special accreditations). To supplement these data, however, other information—often more qualitative than quantitative—is critical. Information on attitudes among faculty within a department regarding new-hire salaries is particularly relevant. For example, although it is generally advisable to resist salary inversion to avoid creating morale problems, there are times when the continuing faculty recognize the need for higher salaries to attract quality hires and are willing to bear such an overlap. Without such qualitative information, vice presidents and deans risk making decisions on initial salaries that may lead to an inability to attract or retain the best new faculty.

Decisions related to annual salary increases involve a number of dimensions, each requiring different types of quantitative and qualitative information. One dimension, except when salary increases are just a fixed percentage across the board, is merit, which involves questions of how merit will be defined, what information is pertinent and reliable, and how that information will be used to make a merit increase decision. Merit-based salary increases typically come from recommendations by department chairs based on their annual evaluations of faculty. This information is usually quantitative, in the form of evaluation ratings, and is guided by specific institutional procedures that combine other pertinent quantitative and qualitative data, such as students' evaluations of faculty, peer evaluations, reviews of faculty productivity, and evidence of service.

However, although the evaluation ratings may be quantitative, they are far from standardized and result in marked differences from one department to another. For example, one department chair, in a desire to boost faculty morale, may give evaluation ratings of "outstanding" to almost all faculty within that department, making only small distinctions between faculty within the "outstanding" range and leaving the real evaluation to the salary recommendations. Another chair may make more significant distinctions in faculty evaluation ratings based on very similar faculty data. Such differences—even when salary increase funds are allocated proportionally to departments based on current salaries—lead to faculty questioning and even distrusting the procedures. For example, faculty in the department where all receive an evaluation of "outstanding" will get only an average increase of, say, 3.5 percent yet learn that faculty in the other department with an "outstanding" rating received an above-average increase of 5 percent. Additional quantitative data will not solve this problem. What is required is a qualitative study involving faculty and department chairs using methods such as case studies and focus groups to better understand the sources of the disparities and to encourage them to identify possible solutions.

Another issue faced with annual salary increases is salary equity within the institution, including possible individual inequities, possible gender inequities, and possible salary compression at particular ranks. To do equity analyses requires pertinent quantitative data including information on current salary, rank, years of service, highest degree, discipline, and evaluation ratings. These data can then be analyzed in two ways to provide useful information. First, multiple regression can be used to determine cases where actual salaries are significantly different from predicted salaries based on a regression equation. This can be useful in identifying potential cases of individual salary inequities, and by looking across such cases, it can be useful in identifying potential gender inequities, provided that gender is not used as a variable in the regression equation. Second, the data can simply be arrayed in tables listing salaries by department, rank, and years of service within rank along with mean salaries by rank for each department. This can be useful in identifying potential cases of salary compression by rank.

Such quantitative data and analyses can identify only potential cases of inequities. To determine whether these cases represent actual inequities, it is essential that the results be reviewed by department chairs and deans to identify possible alternative explanations. For example, even when evaluation ratings are included in a salary regression analysis, those data are typically not reliable enough to capture salary variations due to poor performance in the resulting equation. However, department chairs or deans, in reviewing the regression results, can often identify that a faculty member's history of poor performance explains the discrepancy between the actual and predicted salary and can recognize that this is not an example of an actual individual salary inequity. At the same time, they can recognize when a low increase many years in the past has compounded to the point that it has had a disproportionately negative effect on the current salary.

Academic administrators also should address possible salary inequities across institutions—that is, cases where an institution's salaries have not kept pace in certain disciplines with those at otherwise comparable institutions—as these lagging salaries can have major consequences for faculty retention and morale. Although this is a dimension of faculty compensation that is too often ignored by administrators because of limited funds, it is the dimension that is most frequently noted by faculty. Again, both quantitative and qualitative data are needed for understanding the situation and considering alternative solutions.

Unfortunately, such interinstitutional comparisons are too commonly made using only inadequate quantitative data. It is common for faculty, for example, to compare entry-level salaries in their discipline at their institution with the entry-level salaries at other institutions in their region without regard for type of institution. Further, immediately after the March–April issue of *Academe* is published, it is common for faculty to compare the all-ranks faculty salary average for their institution with the faculty salary average of other comparable institutions. In both of these examples, additional information is needed for adequate comparisons to identify if salaries are really lagging. If a set of peer-group institutions has not been identified for making such comparisons, it is essential that this be done using relevant characteristics that are clearly communicated to faculty and administrators. More information is needed than just the all-ranks faculty salary averages to make appropriate comparisons. There are six major types of differences between faculty salaries when institutions are compared: differences in the type of institution (for example, doctoral versus comprehensive), differences across disciplines (for example, salaries for computer science faculty versus those for English faculty), differences due to faculty rank, differences due to years of service, differences due to individual faculty factors (such as performance history), and differences due to institutional expenditures for salary increases. It is the last source of differences that faculty usually question when making interinstitutional comparisons and that cannot be understood except in the context of competing demands for resources.

We have found it useful, based on data from CUPA on peer-group faculty salaries by discipline and by rank, to create analyses that provide comparisons that control for type of institution, differences across disciplines, and differences due to rank. By also including data on years of service for faculty within each discipline and rank and by relying on department chairs and deans to identify confounding factors related to individual faculty, we have been able to obtain more valid comparisons to support decisions related to salary equity across institutions. Again, however, as with the other examples, such quantitative data only provides part of the information needed. Qualitative information regarding faculty perceptions, academic priorities, and other institutional factors are essential to have adequate information for decision making.

Managing Faculty Workload. Although many faculty handbooks specify the standard teaching load, factors such as reassigned time policies, reductions for administration, graduate teaching responsibilities, class sizes, and grant activities result in differing workload for individuals as well as departments. Many academic administrators use a standard registrar printout to determine whether faculty have full loads and make decisions at the beginning of each semester to cut all classes with low enrollments or combine course sections to save money. Such decision making is seen by faculty as micromanagement and short sighted.

It is not a limitation of the data that makes these decisions questionable but rather the context for understanding faculty workload that is distorted by assumptions. There is no institutional resource difference between a nine-credit load for each faculty member and an average nine-credit load for the unit. Thus, a more appropriate analysis would make neither the course nor the individual faculty member the unit of analysis but rather the department or the program. A faculty member might well carry several large classes to subsidize a low-enrollment specialty class. Several faculty members might teach more than others to support undergraduate research or internship supervision. With different assumptions, the foundation for planning would shift from equity to whether the resources are arrayed to achieve the desired results.

Too often a false notion of equity in teaching loads overwhelms judgments about learning outcomes. Indeed, we have observed campus committees focused on workload issues bog down over dilemmas such as credit hours versus contact hours, how faculty supervision of labs should be measured, what the maximum number should be for clinical supervision in health professions, or how to count private music lessons. The context for reviewing full-time equivalency per faculty member is further clouded by questions of how many preparations the faculty member has, how many days of the week the courses meet, and whether technology or graduate assistants are used for some of the teaching. Faculty reluctantly come to understand that there may be no such thing as clearly defined equity in workloads and that different principles do and should guide faculty assignments.

Recently, public institutions have been faced with state-level analyses of teaching capacity as part of funding formulas. Based on peer-group comparisons with other states, optimal class sizes are established that differ by discipline. Although academic administrators may take some guidance from these teaching capacity models to manage resources carefully, they require considerable additional information from institutional researchers, including accreditation standards, research requirements, teaching assistant resources, faculty dissertation load, and more. Efficiency in course loads is not the only goal, and neither is teaching the only responsibility of faculty.

There is considerable evidence that workload, both personal and professional, does impact overall faculty productivity, especially with regard to research (Creswell, 1985). Because there are significantly different teaching loads even on a single campus, it is clear that not mere numbers of students taught but rather perceptions about one's load are critical to productivity and morale. It takes qualitative measures to get at how faculty manage their time and set priorities to provide guidance for decision makers. Thus, the institutional research office must help design the appropriate qualitative study, perhaps to be conducted by department chairs or the faculty development office, to improve the confidence of faculty who participate. As most institutional research office staffs are small, their expertise should be spent on developing the tools rather than conducting the study and analyzing all the data.

Improving Faculty Performance. The first three issues related to faculty rely heavily on information from institutional research. In contrast, the traditional approach to measuring faculty performance is the annual evaluation of teaching, research, and service activity that is conducted solely by faculty colleagues and department chairs. This example, however, can demonstrate how a partnership with institutional research can improve information that is the basis of the evaluation and promote understanding of this complex area by faculty who are usually quite skeptical about the meaning of such performance evaluations. Faculty may choose to reject the research findings about faculty motivation and productivity (Blackburn, 1995) as too complex or irrelevant to their situation, but they can be sensitized by campus-based studies.

To provide a basis for evaluation, faculty annually list their activities, summarize their student evaluations of teaching, and note the number of publications and presentations. Personnel committees count up the numbers, perhaps make comparisons with others in the department, and rely too often on quantity alone to make recommendations for reappointment, merit salary increase, or even post-tenure review. From time to time a department chair reviews the faculty member's plan for the coming year, asks what resources will be required to accomplish it, and might have the courage to ask whether the faculty member has achieved his or her goals the previous year.

For the board of visitors, accreditors, or others who want evidence of faculty productivity, the counts of publications, citations, or scores on teaching evaluations are often deemed enough to demonstrate the vitality of the faculty. However, the vice president for academic affairs who wants to see a continuously developing faculty will need more than these numbers or a trend report—he or she will need information about the culture of support for improving teaching and increasing research productivity. To assess this dimension—the culture of expectations—the institutional research office must develop ways to link quantitative measures shown to have an impact on faculty productivity, such as work load and numbers of students taught by a particular department, with qualitative measures such as the leadership of the chair, the expectations of the dean, and the norms of the discipline. Many studies show that despite what administrators say they value, faculty know what is rewarded, and it influences their productivity (Creswell, 1986; Diamond, Gray, and Fruh, 1992).

Sometimes interviews and focus groups reveal troubling information such as that in one department the senior faculty discourage junior faculty from publishing, give messages about how teaching is more important, give higher teaching loads to junior faculty, call them rate busters rather than congratulate them on accepted publications, and avoid mentoring relationships, whereas in another department the senior faculty give their travel money to junior faculty, co-author publications to get them started, and monitor teaching loads to ensure a balanced professional life. Obviously, to understand faculty productivity and then influence the conditions that support it, the vice president for academic affairs needs the insight and information that this qualitative research effort provides. Efforts to change the culture cannot be successful if one does not know what is holding the old culture in place or what the disincentives for change are.

Increasing Curricular Productivity. One of the most understudied areas of academic life is the curriculum, and yet it is responsible for the student learning results and captures, through faculty salaries, most of the resources in academic affairs. Standard institutional research approaches provide only minimal information such as number of majors, unenrolled seats, and space utilization. From time to time, customized reports are developed, such as migration studies that show what students thought their major would be and what their ultimate choices are. When new curricula are proposed, additional reports can provide data from environmental scans with regard to job prospects for graduates or potential faculty availability. Because the curriculum is seen as the prerogative of the faculty, there is much less administrative demand for management information than in other aspects of academic affairs. However, two types of studies can provide valuable information regarding the quality and the costs of the curriculum—program review and studies of curricular efficiency.

Making Program Review Effective. Academic program review is the standard process for evaluating the effectiveness and productivity of the curriculum (Barak and Breier, 1990; Barak and Mets, 1995). Whether state mandated or institution specific, the standard criteria are a mix of input measures such as resources available, grant activity, and student demand for the program; output measures such as faculty publications, alumni giving, and employment of graduates; and institutional values such as centrality to the mission of the institution. The institutional research office can begin the process by developing standard data sets for all the units undergoing review that year. As the units begin their work, however, each will call for a variety of tailored studies relevant to their curricular goals to supplement the quantitative measures with qualitative assessments.

Many program reviews require qualitative data such as a history of the program and of the discipline to anchor the future aspirations of the program. They may also use employer feedback, especially in professional programs such as teacher education and nursing, to get a deeper understanding of the perceived quality of the program as represented by its graduates. Some campuses use external reviewers, national ratings, and other quality perceptions to balance the self-reported evaluation by the campus-based faculty. All of this data, qualitative and quantitative, forms the basis for a self-study.

The campus-based process that interprets and makes recommendations based on the self-study is the most powerful part of the program review process. Among the most effective processes are those that use a faculty committee to review the self-study and meet with faculty colleagues in units other than their own to discuss the findings. This has the advantages of providing a critical external perspective that is also anchored by an understanding of the campus as well as ensuring that recommendations for future improvement are relevant and feasible for the campus. The deliberations serve to inform the members of the program review committee so that the base of understanding of curricular quality across the campus increases each year as more faculty are involved. The credibility of the process is also always reviewed because faculty know they will be subject to the same standards in the future and will suggest corrections to aspects of the process that are not productive.

An additional stage that further enhances the impact of program review is when the committee steps back and does a qualitative review of the reviews, looking for common themes that are institutional issues and not just program specific. Among the kinds of themes that emerge may be those related to technology, budget, or facilities—issues that hamper the entire institution and thus require a response from the administration and not from the faculty in the unit being reviewed. Providing this type of perspective is essential for strengthening academic affairs overall and moving program review from a periodic justification of a single program to a future-oriented program development model of value to the entire institution. Clearly, this type of work can benefit from the guidance of institutional researchers but would lose all credibility if faculty were not directly involved.

Investing in Curricular Efficiency. Although faculty are understandably most interested in curricular quality, it is no longer sufficient to justify programs on those measures alone. With severely limited resources, academic administrators must also measure the efficiency of the curriculum. Significant research conducted by Middaugh (2001) can provide important national data on costs of programs and help provide measures of productivity. His study has created a large data set by which a campus can determine, for example, that although all nursing programs are more expensive than sociology programs, their particular nursing program is 10 percent more costly than the reported average. The analyses are based primarily on faculty and staff salaries and provide a fairly simple yardstick of direct costs. Greater efficiency can be achieved when more students are taught with the same resources.

Although most faculty would instinctively argue that increased effectiveness of the curriculum requires more resources, effectiveness and efficiency need not be trade-offs. Complex work in the study of curricular efficiency has been conducted that focuses not only on how to reduce the costs of the curriculum through more efficient use of faculty but also on how to invest in student success to both reduce instructional costs and increase tuition revenues (Ferren and Slavings, 2000). Such analyses link efficiency and effectiveness and argue for not just more students taught but more students who are successful. The analyses look, for example, at the costs of reteaching students when they withdraw or fail courses or the cost of attrition in lost tuition dollars. The analyses suggest strategic investments in support programs based on qualitative assessments of what students need such as supplemental instruction, peer tutoring, freshman seminars, and other interventions that help more students pass courses, stay in college, and graduate on time. When shown the dollars saved by not reteaching students in high-risk courses such as chemistry, computer science, and calculus, many faculty are willing to try supplemental instruction or promote peer-tutoring programs to prevent failures and withdrawals. In short, they see that an investment in effectiveness results in efficiency.

None of these tools are of any value if faculty attitudes do not embrace the idea that all students can learn and that grade distributions need not be a normal curve. Indeed, our campus study of faculty attitudes revealed that the grade report put out each semester, a historical document begun in an era of concern about grade inflation and close monitoring of faculty, made faculty think they would be rewarded for failing students rather than teaching them successfully. Too many A's, they believed, made the faculty member suspect rather than earn recognition for good teaching. Faculty resisted giving students opportunities to rewrite papers or retake exams and derived pride from ignoring student requests for additional help in learning, saying they just need to sink or swim. Simply reorienting the report by course, not faculty member, gave department chairs new insight. In a case such as this, institutional research also has a role in gathering essential qualitative data that defines the context in which faculty decisions are being made, such as information about their students' preferred learning styles or confidence levels of first-generation students. Such information can help change faculty perceptions so that their efforts contribute to alternative pedagogies, realistic evaluation standards, and better curricular performance.

Increasing Student Learning. The assessment of student outcomes has become increasingly important in recent years, both to provide information that has become more and more commonly required by state councils and accrediting agencies and to assist decision makers within an institution in better understanding the real impact of their curricula on students (Banta, 1988). With the increased attention to examining student outcomes, institutional researchers have learned that traditional quantitative outcome assessments—standardized tests and surveys—are not sufficient by themselves to provide all of the information needed; they must be supplemented by qualitative assessments that capture the context of such changes, the relationships between processes and outcomes, and the unintended outcomes that could otherwise be missed. In this section we provide examples of two types of institutional research related to student learning—learning outcomes and student engagement.

Assessing Learning Outcomes. Assessment of student learning has a long history of using a wide variety of quantitative measures, including tests of basic skills and measures of competencies for specific majors through capstone experiences including courses, theses, and exams. Tracking these measures over time provides a campus with a good picture of what students know, how they compare against norms, and how college has added value. Most often these efforts are driven by the expertise of the institutional research office, which helps faculty make selections of evaluation instruments and approaches.

Recently, there has been a shift to outcome measures after completion of college, such as examinations of how many students are employed in their field after graduation and what salaries they command. However, in a high-employment period, such quantitative data are confounded because every student can get a job and employers are pleased initially just to have the position filled. To more fully understand the outcomes of a program, qualitative studies of what employers think of the graduates or the students' capacity for upward mobility as measured by securing a second and third job are more revealing.

Appropriate qualitative data on student learning can also include changes in aspirations, confidence levels of students, and capacity for lifelong learning. Indeed, a whole variety of aspects can be assessed that demonstrate the capacity students have for success independent of the institution. For faculty to appreciate the complexity of assessment, they must be involved in both planning and conducting the studies. Negative views of assessment as just too much work soften when faculty get answers to real questions that they have about how their students learn.

Richard Light's groundbreaking work (1990) at Harvard University involved students as well in the qualitative studies of not just what but how students learn. The students were able to gather information that revealed differences in the ways women and men learn, the different advising relationships women sought with faculty, the way in which students chose courses, and more. Many preconceptions about the disadvantages of being involved in athletics, extracurricular activities, or work were shattered when the data gathered showed students demonstrated more energy, better time management, and better academic performance when they had a balanced life. This type of information provides a valuable context for faculty decisions about course design, pedagogy, and involvement with students.

Increasing Student Engagement. One of the most interesting, yet still not widespread, avenues of research on student success is related to their level of engagement with the campus (Kuh, Schuh, and Whitt, 1991). Although strongly urged by the national study *Involvement in Learning* (National Institute of Education, 1984) to set high standards and develop more engaging pedagogy, faculty have been slow to integrate strategies for active learning, and many classrooms are still based on delivery of material through lectures. Recent work conducted on the impact of faculty expectations on student effort show that patterns of involvement and high expectations must be set early in the first year (Schilling and Schilling, 1999). Campuses that feel a gap between faculty expectations and student expectations would do well to conduct qualitative studies of recruiting materials, orientations, and introductory course syllabi to understand the ways in which the campus inadvertently stresses that college is fun rather a challenge. Faculty might be more likely then to directly encourage students to set high goals rather than lament their perceived laziness.

A review of standard quantitative studies conducted by institutional research offices on most campuses about students would show good information about their ratings of advising, their perceptions of safety in the residence halls, and whether they like the food. Few standard studies ask students how many hours a week they study, how much they read, and how many times they seek help from their instructors. There is even less information about what motivates students, what distracts them, and what makes them avoid full engagement with the campus.

Based on the well-researched principles of the importance of both challenge and support for student success, the National Study of Student Engagement (NSSE) addresses the many levels at which a student can be involved with the activities of the campus, with other students, and with faculty. The 2000 NSSE survey was conducted on freshmen and seniors on 276 campuses and reports data in five categories—level of academic challenge, active and collaborative learning, student interaction with faculty members, enriching educational experiences, and supportive campus environment. This type of quantitative data allows a campus to compare its students' experience with those at similar institutions and provides an important backdrop for additional qualitative work on a campus.

Our campus, for example, discovered that the significant attention paid to freshmen resulted in higher-than-average scores on all dimensions, showing that our efforts to help them connect with the campus were successful. In contrast, those higher levels of connection were not matched by the results from seniors. We are now challenged to determine whether we were less intentional in previous years or whether our efforts were not continued and the initial effects eroded. The Institutional Research Office is helping a faculty group design studies not only to better understand the student experience but also to plan intentional efforts to help students assume greater and greater responsibility for their own learning as they progress from freshmen to graduates. Both quantitative and qualitative work will be necessary to assess the results of a variety of community-building efforts that engage faculty and staff as well as students in activities aimed at impacting student learning in both curricular and cocurricular settings. Based on the work to date, it is clear that the faculty will also be strong advocates with the administration for appropriate recognition and rewards for faculty and staff whose work directly impacts increased student engagement.

Implications for the Roles of Institutional Research and Academic Administration

As it is highly unlikely that campuses will be able to expand their institutional research staff to meet the many new challenges in academic administration, not just the role of the academic administrator but also that of the institutional researcher may well need to change. Institutional research can no longer be treated as a free good or as the sole keeper of information. Understandably, to stretch limited resources, institutional researchers on many campuses are making databases available for others to analyze. Further, they are holding discussions among key administrators about who the institutional research office serves and the foundation activities expected to manage the institution well. Similarly, academic administrators no longer rely on others to do data analyses or believe that a few quick calculations coupled with experience and intuition will lead to good and defensible decisions. They are selecting staff not just for their knowledge of academic affairs but also based on their technical skills.

To facilitate this more focused, streamlined research capability, academic administrators must be selective in what they want to know and screen access to the institutional research office. To keep faculty from feeling they are having their access to information controlled, academic administrators will need to work with faculty in setting agendas for institutional research to address key questions, including these: Which questions are critical to understanding our current situation? What information will improve our planning efforts? Which studies will tell us how we are succeeding in those efforts?

In addition, both administrators and faculty will need to agree on the fundamental purposes of institutional research. Realistically, studies should be conducted only if actions are to be taken. Academic administrators must make hundreds of decisions and need useful, but not always exhaustive, data to support those decisions. Researchers need to recognize that not all studies need to be elegant, and sometimes the simplest approach should be taken to get the information needed. Timelines should be set at the outset so that studies do not delay decisions. In the end, not every management decision or planning effort must be supported by complex annual institutional research—the challenge is to recognize and support those few critical decisions in specific areas that will shape the future of the institution.

In this environment, the institutional research office will still need to maintain the basic factbooks and databases but will also, in consultation with academic affairs, need to make judicious decisions about participation in important national studies such as the Higher Education Research Institute faculty survey and NSSE to provide a broader context for institutional data. Further, institutional researchers will still need to have the high-level technical skills to link many databases for internal studies that give greater meaning to such matters as faculty workload, retention, and student satisfaction. To extend their reach, however, they must be willing to train others—including staff in academic affairs—to do some of the analyses. Finally, institutional researchers must be able to design studies that supplement quantitative information with qualitative information from focus groups, interviews, and content analysis of documents to address key concerns related to faculty, students, and the curriculum. They must be able to train faculty, graduate students, and administrators to conduct some of the data collection and analysis. In short, every effort should be made to hand off the routine activities, expand the number of individuals knowledgeable in institutional research, and consult regularly with key administrators to pare down the work so that the merely interesting questions take low priority compared to the essential studies.

References

Banta, T. W. (ed.) *Implementing Outcomes Assessment: Promise and Perils.* San Francisco: Jossey-Bass, 1988.

Barak, R. J., and Breir, B. E. *Successful Program Review: A Practical Guide to Evaluating Programs in Academic Settings.* San Francisco: Jossey-Bass, 1990.

Barak, R. J., and Mets, L. A. *Using Academic Program Review.* New Directions for Institutional Research, no. 86. San Francisco: Jossey-Bass, 1995.

Blackburn, R. T. *Faculty at Work: Motivation, Expectation, and Satisfaction.* Baltimore: Johns Hopkins University Press, 1995.

Creswell, J. W. "Faculty Research Performance: Lessons from the Sciences and Social Sciences." In A. J. Seagren, J. W. Creswell, and D. W. Wheeler (eds.), *The Department Chair: New Roles, Responsibilities, and Challenges.* ASHE/ERIC Research Reports, vol. 22, no. 1. Washington, D.C.: Association for the Study of Higher Education, 1985.

Creswell, J. W. (ed.). *Measuring Faculty Research Performance.* New Directions for Institutional Research, no. 50. San Francisco: Jossey-Bass, 1986.

Cyert, R. M., Simon, H. M., and Trow, D. B. "Observation of a Business Decision." In Herbert A. Simon (ed.), *Models of Bounded Rationality,* Vol. 2: *Behavioral Economics and Business Organization.* Cambridge, Mass.: MIT Press, 1983.

Diamond, R. M., Gray, P. J., and Fruh, R. C. *The National Study of Research Universities and the Balance between Research and Undergraduate Teaching.* Syracuse, N.Y.: Center for Instructional Development, Syracuse University, 1992.

Ewell, P. T. "Information for Decision: What's the Use?" In P. T. Ewell (ed.), *Enhancing Information Use in Decision Making.* New Directions for Institutional Research, no. 64. San Francisco: Jossey-Bass, 1989.

Ferren, A. S., and Slavings, R. *Investing in Quality: Tools for Improving Curricular Efficiency.* Washington, D.C.: Association of American Colleges and Universities, 2000.

Kuh, G. D., Schuh, J. H., and Whitt, E. J. *Involving Colleges: Successful Approaches to Fostering Student Learning and Development Outside the Classroom.* San Francisco: Jossey-Bass, 1991.

Light, R. J. *The Harvard Assessment Seminars: Explorations with Students and Faculty about Teaching, Learning, and Student Life.* Cambridge, Mass.: Harvard Graduate School of Education, 1990.

Middaugh, M. *Understanding Faculty Productivity: Standards and Benchmarks for Colleges and Universities.* San Francisco: Jossey-Bass, 2001.

National Institute of Education. *Involvement in Learning: Realizing the Potential of American Higher Education.* Washington, D.C.: U.S. Government Printing Office, 1984.

Schilling, K. M., and Schilling, K. L. "Increasing Expectations for Student Efforts." *About Campus,* 1999, 4(2), 4–10.

ANN S. FERREN is vice president for academic affairs and professor of educational studies at Radford University. Her research and publications focus on general education, efficiency of the curriculum, faculty development, and academic leadership.

MARTIN S. AYLESWORTH is coordinator of assessment in the institutional research office and associate professor of educational studies at Radford University. His major research interests are in the area of assessment in higher education and the assessment of critical thinking skills.

6

A systems approach that builds a rich context from multiple perspectives for decision making using quantitative and qualitative data is valuable to presidents in reaching the final answer.

The Use of Quantitative and Qualitative Information in Institutional Decision Making

Mark L. Perkins

As an institutional researcher twenty-five years ago, I often wondered what happened to those extraordinary reports and fantastic studies prepared by our office when they hit the decision-making process in the president's office. Ray Stata, president and chief executive officer of Analog Devices, Inc., in an interview with Peter Senge, has suggested that "there is a tremendous tendency of people high in the organization to become remote from reality and the facts, to begin to hypothesize and conjecture without any formal grounding of their theories" (Senge, 1990, p. 351). As chancellor, I now receive numerous reports and studies from throughout the institution. Many provide me with interesting information, but few focus on the significant leadership questions, challenges, and opportunities the institution needs to address. Years ago when I sent those quantitative studies to the president, it was so clear what could be done about retention, how the budget could be balanced, and that athletics was an economic burden. Now as a university chancellor some years and a few gray hairs later, I have a perspective to share on the rest of the story.

When I reflected on my experience as a chancellor in using quantitative and qualitative data in the decision-making process, I was shocked by how the pace of the office and role of chancellor can mask how operating and strategic decisions are actually made. As a strategic thinker who believes plans grounded in data and informed by the environment are the key to success, I was surprised by how much reflection was needed to understand my personal approach to decision making. For example, are there really two different kinds of decisions: qualitative and quantitative? How is data used

New Directions for Institutional Research, no. 112, Winter 2001 © John Wiley & Sons, Inc.   85

in making a presidential decision? What are the roles of the chancellor or president and the institutional researcher in the decision-making process?

Quantitative and Qualitative Decisions

Are there really quantitative decisions and qualitative decisions, or are there simply decisions informed by qualitative and quantitative data? In musing on this question with my colleague James Fisher, who is a scholar on the U.S. College and University Presidency, he reflected that "every decision is ultimately a qualitative one" (personal communication, July 2000). This insight suggests that there are not really two distinct kinds of decisions but rather decisions or judgments made using quantitative and qualitative inputs. Most important, he sees every decision as ultimately using qualitative inputs.

Let's consider as an example the selection of a new employee. The hiring decision begins with a simple review of data such as whether the candidates have the appropriate degree or meet minimum job requirements. It evolves to a quantitative evaluation of experience such as years of service, size of budget managed, number of people supervised, and so on. Ultimately the decision moves to the highly contextual questions of the candidate's fit with the organization, which is qualitative and involves concerns such as management style, personality, communication skills, demeanor, and the like. Thus, if we look at the hiring of a new employee as a single decision, we see it involves multiple judgments and requires information from simple facts to quantitative and qualitative assessments ranging from experience to organizational fit. These inputs, when linked together, provide knowledge about the candidate pool and a context for reflecting on candidates as potential employees based on the decision maker's understanding of the needs and culture of the organization. In the end it is this reflection by the decision maker that makes every decision a qualitative one. The ultimate hiring decision is a qualitative judgment based on quantitative and qualitative inputs that provide a context for understanding and reaching a final decision.

The selection process serves as a system for building a decision-making context, as do other institutional processes such as planning, budgeting, and so on. The selection process moves from a focus on the individual to that individual in the context of other candidates and then to those candidates in the context of the organization. In this process, as Senge (1990) suggests we develop "the capability of seeing the forest *and* the trees—of seeing information in terms of broad and detailed patterns" (p. 135). In essence, we move from a smaller context to a larger and more complex context—the bigger picture. Upon reflection I know that in making decisions as chancellor I regularly follow this progression because it results in a context, or what Senge calls a *mental model,* for decision making. For Senge mental models are "assumptions, generalizations, or even pictures or images that influence how we understand the world and how we take action" (p. 8). I see presidential leadership as building a context or mental model for making sense out of the world so that we can determine what institutional actions are most appropriate. In the end, presidential decisions are qualitative judgments formed by reflecting on a mental model or decision-making context built from the relationships among a vast array of quantitative and qualitative inputs. It is this insight that I needed most as an institutional researcher oh those many years ago. Much of what I gave the president in those days was empirical in nature and came most often from a limited perspective without any qualitative data to enrich the context. How much more effective I could have been had I seen my role as that of helping build a broad context for institutional decision making grounded in quantitative and qualitative inputs from multiple perspectives.

Building Context: A Mental Model for Decision Making

Institutional researchers can be the most helpful to decision makers by assisting them in developing that mental model or rich context for decision making. Such a context can foster an understanding of key relationships among quantitative and qualitative inputs that are essential for the multiple judgments that lead to a final decision. To build such a context or model, it is helpful to understand how data, information, and knowledge work together and lead to understanding. (See Figure 6.1.)

A data element such as a quantitative single number or qualitative student perception is a simple fact when we capture it, and standing alone, it offers limited information. When we link it to other data elements, it begins to build a context and becomes information. For example, this year's headcount enrollment increases in meaning when it is placed in the

Figure 6.1. Elements of a Mental Model for Decision Making

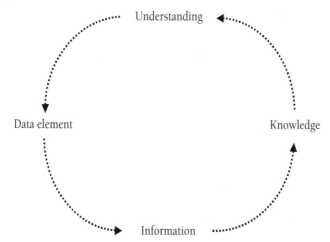

context of last year's enrollment or for that matter the enrollment of the previous decade. Similarly, qualitative expressions such as a student's perception of key features of our university increases in meaning when placed in the context of last year's student's expressions or that of other students in the same class. Institutional researchers are very good at identifying linkages within groups of captured data such as enrollment and faculty data over time. Institutional fact books are classic examples of efforts to create information for our colleges and universities. As chancellor I find them to be a necessary foundation yet limited in providing knowledge and understanding.

As we increase the linkages among, and especially between, data elements, we achieve a richer context and gain knowledge from these multiple relationships. For example, when we relate student applications to admissions and ultimately to student enrollment, we gain knowledge about the demand for and perhaps the desirability of our institution. When we relate conversations with parents and students to our quantitative information, we increase the richness of the context and add to our understanding of the effectiveness of our student recruitment and enrollment efforts. In reflecting on this emerging context or mental model, we include our own experience and begin to achieve understanding. According to Senge and others (1990), "You can't live your life without adding meaning or drawing conclusions. It would be an inefficient, tedious way to live. But you can improve your communications through reflection" (p. 245). To help us do this, he offers the following: "(1) Become more aware of your own thinking and reasoning (reflection); (2) Make your thinking and reasoning more visible to others (advocacy); (3) Inquire into other's thinking and reasoning (inquiry)" (p. 245). This approach has helped me develop mental models that are useful for identifying strategic opportunities for my university and in reaching major institutional decisions.

The context, or mental model–building process, works for both quantitative and qualitative data. Relationships built through linkages result in a rich context for reflection and decision making. Figure 6.2 is a graphic representation of this process.

In this iterative process we capture data, make linkages, and reflect to generate information, knowledge, and understanding. As we do so, we enrich the context for decision making as suggested in Figure 6.3.

The iterative process of developing linkages and reflection is critical to building a rich context for decision making. In this context-building process, I found communication between decision makers and the institutional researcher to be paramount for our effectiveness. In fact, this process of mental model development was greatly facilitated by two things: complete academic freedom for the chancellor and the institutional researcher and physical proximity.

It is strange to assert the need for academic freedom for a university's leader, but it is essential in the mental model–building process. Virtually

Figure 6.2. Mental Model-Building Process

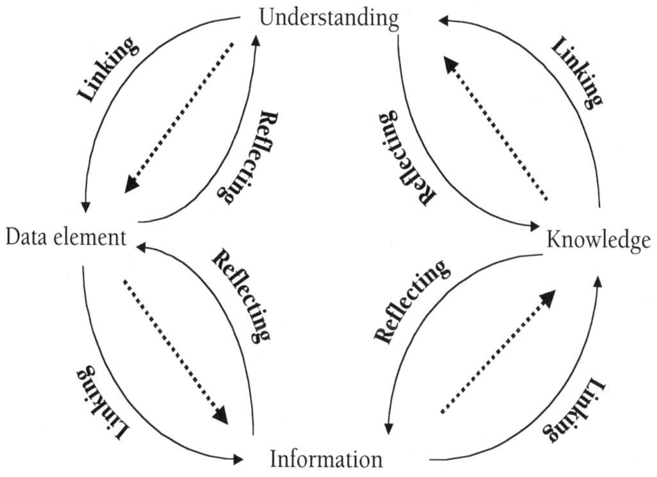

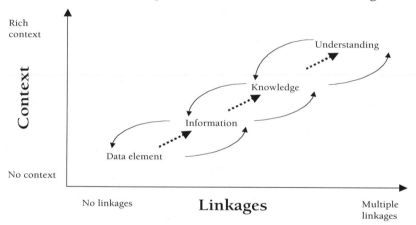

Figure 6.3. Building a Mental Model for Decision Making

every utterance of a university chancellor or president can be misconstrued as policy or a call to specific action. The president or chancellor in this process must be free to make his or her perspectives, interests, values, thinking, and reasoning visible to the staff assisting in developing the context or mental model for decision making. The institutional researcher must also have the freedom to challenge this thinking and articulate options for further reflection. This important communication was greatly facilitated for me because the institutional researcher is located in close proximity to my office.

Context development, then, is an iterative process that must include the values, interests, and perspectives of the decision maker if it is to advance the decision maker's understanding of various options and opportunities. Developing an effective context for decision making requires regular communication with those responsible for supporting the context development process.

Communication and Iteration in Context Development

In fall 1998 the faculty senate at the University of Wisconsin–Green Bay challenged me as chancellor to think strategically about our academic program and the position of our campus and university. This was especially exciting for me because the faculty indicated a willingness to explore new possibilities. Little did we understand at the time where such thinking might lead.

I translated this faculty request into two fundamental questions that drove my exploration of our university's position. First, who are we? And second, where can we go? Beginning with the first, I asked our institutional researcher to describe for me in basic terms who we are as an institution from her perspective. Right away she said we were a public four-year comprehensive university, which of course was how we are classified under the Carnegie system and within the University of Wisconsin System. I mused about this with her and wondered how we stacked up among all public universities. Soon I received an analysis showing we were among 501 four-year public universities nationwide and were in the largest category—the comprehensives—consisting of 272, or 54 percent, of the public institutions. After reflecting on this, I wondered how we compared to comprehensive universities in other ways—for example, in enrollment, program offerings, and master's degrees awarded per year, which is the basis for our classification as a comprehensive university. More information in a broader context was generated; we learned that our enrollment was significantly below average for a comprehensive, that we offered twenty-two fewer degree programs than the average for comprehensive universities even in our own system, and that we rarely awarded the twenty master's degrees required to qualify as a comprehensive university. After reflecting on our university from the perspective of classification, I wondered how we might be viewed by the consumers: students and their parents. We turned our attention to the most prevalent commercial source of information about U.S. colleges and universities, *The U.S. News and World Report* ranking data. What an interesting experience it was to organize that data by state and learn about the institutional choices available across the United States. The first analysis I viewed showed there were only doctoral and comprehensive universities in the state of Wisconsin. Our campus was among the eleven comprehensives. Analysis of other states in the Midwest and states with similar populations revealed that two-thirds of those states had at least three types of institutions: doctoral, comprehensive, and baccalaureate, thus giving more choices for their citizens. Given our nationally distinctive interdisciplinary problem-focused approach to teaching and learning, our enrollment, and our program array, we seemed to be much more like a liberal arts or baccalaureate institution than a comprehensive university. So much for the simple question of who we are?

This was not the perception held by most members of our university community. They thought of us as a comprehensive university. W. Edward Deming used to say, "No theory, no learning." "If we cannot express our assumptions explicitly in ways that others can understand and build upon, there can be no larger process of testing those assumptions and building public knowledge" (Senge, 1990, p. xix). I knew it would take a lot of dialogue with the university community to achieve a common understanding of who we actually are so we could begin exploring where we might go.

This initial understanding was not achieved based on a simple analysis of data. It resulted from exploratory data analysis shaped by reflection and the curiosities emerging from dialogue with the institutional researcher about findings at each step of the process. At each step or iteration in the context-building process, we added to the information, and that ultimately produced the knowledge base that strongly suggested we were not really a comprehensive university. Iterative exploratory data analysis and dialogue with the chancellor were critical to the development of this mental model for strategic institutional reflection and decision making.

Thinking about how to position the university in the future required us to expand our mental model through reflection. Based on these qualitative judgments, we began to understand our strategic opportunities. This effort followed the same process of iterative, exploratory data analysis used to understand who we were as an institution. Ongoing conversations with institutional leadership were important in building new linkages with other colleges and universities by using inputs from a variety of sources. From these conversations we shaped a broader context by organizing this data by state and type of institution within each state. This work provided us with a new mental model for thinking about our institution within our state, the Carnegie, and *U.S. News and World Report* categories as well as within the country.

Reflection on this new model revealed that we had established a framework for raising important public policy questions about higher education in our state while identifying a potential best-fit market niche that fit our institutional strengths. This additional exploratory analysis confirmed the findings of our earlier work and provided a context for understanding the strategic possibility of becoming the only public tier 1 or 2 baccalaureate institution in the Midwest.

It was now time to share this new context or model for thinking about our university with others to see if they could see the fit and the strategic opportunity before us. This step in building a decision-making context is what Senge and others (1990) describe as "making our thinking processes visible, to see what the differences are in our perceptions and what we have in common" (p. 246). Through this dialogue, we enriched the context and our understanding of the challenges and advantages of pursuing a strategic position as a public baccalaureate university. From this effort we added much qualitative data regarding faculty, staff, and student perceptions of the opportunity as well as their concerns.

Positioning the university as a public baccalaureate university was of concern to many because their context for understanding a baccalaureate university was different. Their mental model suggested we might be moving away from our commitment to existing professional programs and our limited graduate offerings. Once they understood this was not our intent and that the model revealed that 54 percent of the public liberal arts institutions offer master's degrees, the university community agreed we should pursue public baccalaureate status to place us in the distinctive group of eighty-one public institutions in the United States. From our dialogue it was clear that achieving this new position would require new resources and an enhanced learning experience to produce the results needed to attract the public financial support for our efforts.

The final decision to pursue a new strategic position for our university was driven by both quantitative and qualitative categorizations that were shaped in a process of iterative, exploratory data analysis. This strategic work evolved from a close working relationship between the chancellor and the institutional researcher, who shared a focus on developing a model and rich context for decision making. This relationship has been vital to much of the successful work of the university.

The Institutional Researcher and the Context-Building Process

Hindsight is 20/20! Twenty-five years ago I completed lots of studies, some of which may never have made it to the president's office. Now I know that most of them, although major projects for me, were simply informational items prepared without an understanding of the institutional questions on the president's mind or the particular leadership challenges that he was trying to address. As I was exposed to the institutional decision-making context, my analytical capacities became of greater value to the university, my contributions to the university grew, and my career blossomed. As my institutional researcher said just recently, the better she understands the context of the questions I am grappling with as chancellor, the more effective she can be in helping me develop a mental model for decision making. The work of the institutional research office is of greatest value when it enhances the major planning and decision-making processes of the institution by helping leadership develop a rich quantitative and qualitative decision-making context. Clarifying the relationship and role of institutional research in leadership processes is important to increasing quality decision making and institutional effectiveness. The placement of the institutional research function within the organization, the capacity of the institutional research office to develop multiple contextual maps, the orientation of the chief executive to using data in building a mental model for decision making, and the chief executive's willingness to work directly with institutional research in building a rich context for decision making are important considerations.

In many of our organizations, institutional research is not closely linked with the key planning and decision-making processes of the institution. Often institutional research is viewed as the repository of data and information—the responder to external and internal inquiries regarding statistical data and information about the university. Although this is an important function, it alone does not take advantage of the capacity to build a rich context for the critical planning and decision making processes of the institution.

Many times presidents seek reports and analyses much like those cited at the beginning of this chapter without providing a context for how they intend to use them and how they might be focused to enrich the decision-making process. As a moderately sized university, we have a relatively flat organization, with the chancellor's office in close proximity to all of the administrative offices, including institutional research. This facilitates direct collaborative work with institutional research and enhances the quality of the exploratory data analysis in response to the interests and needs of the chancellor in building a context for understanding operational and strategic institutional opportunities.

This relationship allows me to work dynamically and collaboratively with our institutional researcher and increases the effectiveness of our dialogue. This relationship eliminates the need for multiple translations of the work of the researcher and gives me, as chancellor, the opportunity to gain from spontaneous exploratory work that would not typically be found in a formal report passed through a director of institutional research to a vice president and then on to me. I have found that a collaborative working relationship between executive leadership and the institutional research function facilitates the use of both quantitative and qualitative data in the development of a rich context for decision making. It also raises questions worthy of presidential reflection regarding how to take advantage of the capacity of institutional researchers in building such a context:

1. Where is institutional research located in the organization?

2. Is the office physically and organizationally in reasonable proximity to the office of the president to promote collaborative and integrative thinking?

3. Is institutional research viewed simply as a reporting function that produces reports and studies, or is it viewed as having the capacity to assist institutional leadership in developing a rich context for decision making?

4. How does the president view his or her role and responsibility in building a rich context for decision making?

5. Does the institutional research staff have the skills, aptitudes, and resources to support mental model development?

My role and relationship with institutional research has been vital to our efforts in identifying a distinctive future for our university in the University of Wisconsin System and the Midwest.

The Presidential Decision

Presidential decisions are essentially no different from the choices and determinations we make as individuals every day. They are informed by empirical data as well as by the perceptions of our friends and colleagues and ultimately are grounded in a mental model developed from life experiences. Some decisions may be arrived at instantaneously, such as whether we will attend a particular event or make a change on our calendar. Even those decisions are grounded in a mental model that includes our personal or institutional leadership context. The university president's mental decision-making model is broad and consists of multiple perspectives such as those of faculty, trustees, students, community, staff, and in significant ways, families. These multiple perspectives provide a rich context for reflection that leads to understanding and a final judgment.

The iterative dynamics suggested in Figure 6.3 for building a mental model views context development as a system for constructing a framework for decision making. It acknowledges the journey to a final decision as one of multiple judgments leading to a context that fosters understanding. Indeed, it is much like the process we see contestants use on the popular television game show "Who Wants to Be a Millionaire?" On this show, contestants are asked questions, and if they are unsure of the answer, they can ask for assistance from the audience or a friend. Contestants sometimes immediately know the answer based on their existing mental model. Sometimes they seek advice from others to eliminate options and focus on fewer choices. Sometimes their final answer depends as much on intuition as hard facts. Facts and mental models based on our past experience will not always help us decide where we are going! Sometimes we must develop new mental models or contexts for decision making. The selection of the preferred context or mental model to support a decision-making process is a qualitative judgment.

As a chancellor I have sometimes been quite surprised by both the quantitative and qualitative data assembled for my reflection. I have been greatly informed by the qualitative data that helps me understand the perceptions, attitudes, and feelings of our community regarding the strategic issues and concerns of our campus. Thus, being open minded and willing to look at the broader perspective has always been valuable in driving our efforts to build a context for strategic choices for our university. I was surprised to learn from our institutional researcher that what has been most helpful to her in developing a context for decision making was understanding my passions and the possibilities I see for the university. Those passions, commitments, and beliefs have provided her with a framework for testing my hypotheses regarding various alternatives that might be available for us as a campus community. Of course, we rejected a number of those beliefs and values along the way because the qualitative and quantitative information did not support my thinking. Although my professional background may facilitate my ability to frame questions addressable through the use of data, I genuinely believe the opportunity to engage in dialogue with others greatly shaped the direction of our exploratory data analysis and led to a rich mental model for thinking about the future alternatives for our university.

The Rest of the Story

The president's work is about developing an institutional perspective and context for decision making. In my early years I provided a variety of studies and analyses for the president that were much like viewing a single pixel on the computer screen. As chancellor I naturally have the opportunity to see more pixels at a time, and this view influences my perspective. A broader view helps one see the athletic budget in the context of the entire institution. As perspective broadens, the positive impact of the athletic program on the image and recognition of the institution comes into view. Something as simple as understanding that the women's basketball team ranks second in the nation academically among all Division I colleges and universities adds to the mental model. This broader context, upon reflection, provides a different perspective on the budget challenges faced by the athletic program by introducing the positive institutional contributions of the program for our students and the university. The same can be said for those simple analyses of student retention and budget shortfalls that I prepared for the president in those early years. When placed in a rich context, we can see the rest of the story.

When I encouraged him to continue his candidacy for the state legislature, Brad Bates, former mayor of Turlock, California, said to me that the perception of the fish on the hook is significantly different from that of the rest of the school (personal communication, June 1991). So, too, is the perspective of the president. That's why, in the end, a systems approach that builds a rich context for decision making using quantitative and qualitative data is valuable to presidents in reaching that final answer.

References

Senge, P. M. *The Fifth Discipline: The Art and Practice of the Learning Organization.* New York: Currency Doubleday, 1990.
Senge, P. M., Kleiner, A., Roberts, C., Ross, R. B., and Smith, B. J. *The Fifth Discipline Fieldbook.* New York: Currency Doubleday, 1990.

At the time of writing MARK L. PERKINS *was chancellor of the University of Wisconsin–Green Bay and professor of business administration and human development. Currently he is president of Towson University.*

7

Qualitative and quantitative measurements, developed within the context of the values, vision, mission, processes, and outcomes of an institution, are the basic ingredients for informed decision making.

Qualitative and Quantitative Measures: One Driver of a Quality Culture

Jonathan D. Fife

Decision making, as described in the two preceding chapters, reflects a concern on the part of the decision makers that their decisions are not only right but also consistent with meeting the needs of the institution and its stakeholders. In each chapter, the authors discuss the use of integrated qualitative and quantitative information to support their planning and decision making. These decision-making processes reflect many of the attributes associated with the quality movement that many institutions have embraced during the past fifteen years. The intent of these efforts has been to create an organization that reflects quality in all aspects of its programs and processes.

This chapter discusses the characteristics of a quality organization. Various relationships and processes will be examined that contribute to an institution achieving its stated objectives, meeting stakeholder expectations, and being consistently true to its values. In particular, the crucial role that measurement—both qualitative and quantitative—plays in ensuring that these ends are met is the focus of this discussion. This chapter is not necessarily about total quality management, continuous quality improvement, or other derivations of these concepts, although what will be reviewed does pertain to these approaches.

The Drivers of a Quality Institution

Measurement is one of the three drivers essential to developing, maintaining, and modifying an institution's policies and procedures to produce an organizational culture of quality. It is critical to know that without measurement, the other two drivers could not be effectively put in place. The three drivers of a systematic approach to quality are as follows.

Having Shared Vision, Mission, and Concept of Expected Outcomes. All higher education institutions are social institutions. They are granted their existence by a state because they are involved in activities that contribute to the welfare of the citizens of that state. With the founding of Harvard in 1636, the English undergraduate college model, with its classical curriculum, was the accepted norm until the mid-1800s. At this time, research-oriented graduate schools based on the German model and a more applied curriculum promoted through the Morrill Land Grant Act of 1862 began to appear across the nation.

Prior to World War II, all U.S. higher education institutions had two things in common: their size and overall importance to society. As for their size, all were small. This had a major advantage in creating a shared concept of their vision and mission; everyone knew each other and interacted frequently enough to develop a common understanding of the values, vision, and mission of the institution. This created a sense of shared purpose that in turn contributed to consistent outcomes. As for the external importance of a higher education institution, except for the status of its existence in the local community, it held very little meaning to most citizens. A higher education degree was not seen as vital to an individual's personal success or to the economic prosperity of a state and, therefore, there were few external demands on an institution.

In the 1950s and 1960s conditions changed dramatically so that existing assumptions and processes no longer worked. Higher education institutions, especially public institutions, became so large that often it was a problem to know all one's colleagues in the department, let alone the entire institution. This in itself would not have been a problem if society's expectations of higher education institutions remained constant. This did not happen. Higher education institutions began to be seen as being vital to an individual's social mobility and career success, indispensable to the economic well-being of a state, and major players in the nation's long-term research objectives. The positive result of this new importance was that federal, state, and local governments provided increasingly greater financial support. The negative result was that with the money came increased expectations and a concern about how well higher education institutions were meeting society's needs (Crowder and Janosik, 2001).

Thus, the first driver of a quality institution is its ability to have processes that create a shared understanding throughout the organization of who its major stakeholders are and what their needs and expectations are.

Leadership Systems. With the change of institutional size and increased social importance came a need to change how an institution is led. It was always the responsibility of a college president to create a shared understanding of who the internal and external stakeholders of an institution were and to develop and maintain processes that were needed to successfully meet these stakeholders' needs and expectations. When an institution was small and the external demands on the curriculum stable, one person could successfully lead an institution. However, with institutional growth and rapid change in demands on the curriculum, there developed a need to move from a command-and-control style of leadership to a leadership system that functioned throughout the entire institution.

This leadership system has a top-down responsibility to ensure that everyone in the institution understands his or her various individual roles and how these roles contribute to the larger vision and mission of the unit and the institution. As the leadership system works to create this sense of shared vision and mission, it has the bottom-up responsibility of ensuring that the policies and processes of the institution support the mission of each individual. An institution functions best when both the articulated vision and mission of the institution and its policies and procedures work together to meet the needs and expectations of its internal and external stakeholders.

Thus, the second driver of a quality institution is to have leadership systems that reflect both top-down and bottom-up responsibilities.

The issue is, how does an institution's leadership know when this is or is not happening? To answer this requires the third driver of quality.

Contextual Measurement. The old saying "You value what you measure and you measure what you value" is both accurate and incomplete. Too often, what is measured is determined as much by convenience as it is by importance. For example, for many faculty members, refereed publications are considered more critical to their ability to gain tenure than is the quality of their teaching. The reason for this is not that publishing is more highly valued than teaching but that counting the number of refereed publications (a quantitative measurement) is easier than developing indicators of high-quality teaching (a qualitative measurement).

The ease-versus-importance dilemma in measurement is exacerbated by two other conditions. The first is the failure to present data and information in a way that clearly reflects the relationships between what is being measured and the purpose of the measurement. It is only when data and information are placed in the context of what is being examined that their meaning becomes apparent. Deming (1982) made this point in his discussion of profound knowledge when he observed that without context, data and information are merely unimportant numbers and letters.The second condition is that the most common points measured are inputs and outputs. This is partially the consequence of higher education's reliance on the resource model, which guides funding throughout the institution. The primary principle behind this model is that if the campus controls for inputs (for example, accept only the brightest students, hire the best faculty, and maintain an up-to-date infrastructure) and outputs (for example, only graduate students with the highest grades or tenure faculty with the most refereed publications), the result will be a quality institution. What is missing in these measurements is a sense of the real meaning behind the numbers and letters that occurs when the relationships between the numbers and letters are examined in context to the vision and mission of the institution.

Thus, the third driver of a quality institution is to measure both the quantitative inputs and outputs and the qualitative context in which they are measured.

What follows in this chapter are illustrations of how measuring the elements that make up a system of quality will greatly aid in developing a more meaningful presentation of contextual information that can be used to help institutions in the achievement of their vision and mission.

A Systematic Approach to Measuring Quality Processes

Because the needs and expectations of an institution's stakeholders are determined by many considerations, often not directly related to the institution, the measurement of quality is not static. Because the ability of an institution to continuously meet these changing needs determines the quality of an institution, the most meaningful measurements of quality are those that assess the relationships among inputs, processes, and outcomes over a period of time in a way that can be used to help an institution adapt to the changing needs of their stakeholders. Knowing how to develop these measurements is made easier by understanding the three elements of quality: the principles of a quality culture, the values of a quality process, and the criteria of a quality system.

The Principles of a Quality Culture. In an extensive analysis of the literature on quality, Freed, Klugman, and Fife (1997) came to three conclusions. First, there are eight principles that are central to creating a quality organizational culture. Second, these principles form a system that is sequential, interrelated, and interdependent. Put another way, all eight principles must be present to create an organizational culture of quality and without the presence of the preceding principle, the next principle cannot be fully developed. Third, these principles are not only fundamentally compatible with traditional higher education values but also are being practiced at many institutions. However, few institutions are aware of the importance of their order and interdependence. These principles and their relationships to each other are depicted in Figure 7.1.

For these principles to be fully operational in a higher education institution, it is necessary that an institution understand the following points:

• The vision, mission, and expected outcomes of quality organizations are defined by the needs and expectations of the primary internal and external stakeholders.

• How well the expected outcomes are achieved depends on how well the institution's processes and systems are designed to interrelate and support each other in working toward supporting the overall vision, mission, and expected outcomes of the organization.

• Its leadership must recognize that the concept of quality is as much an organizational philosophy and culture as it is a management technique and

Figure 7.1. The Principles of a Quality Culture

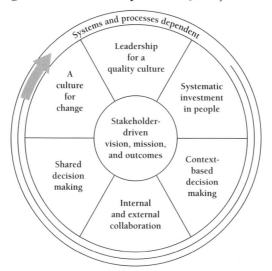

that the culture of an organization is greatly affected by the consistency and integrity between the stated vision of the organization and the processes of the organization. Therefore, there is a top-down responsibility of leadership to create a sense of shared vision and expectations throughout the organization and a bottom-up responsibility to make sure that the processes are aligned with the inherent values of the organization's vision.

• Consistent quality is ensured only when the people in the organization are adequately trained, have some decision-making control over their job, and have a sense of appreciation for their role in the organization. Because no organization succeeds in having quality outcomes if its people are not willing to produce them, a systematic investment in people is the foundation for a quality organization. The single factor that separates the long-term quality companies from their lesser competitors is that they devote more time and money to their people.

• Quality decisions are made consistently, over a long period of time, only when there is an accessible flow of contextual information. One of the major early mistakes organizations make when they begin to institute a quality approach is the use of measurements that are unrelated to the vision, mission, and expected outcomes of the organization and to the processes and systems that are producing the measured results.

• There must be a systematic sharing of information and viewpoints between both internal and external stakeholders to more fully understand the issues and expectations around a problem. Also, by designing processes that foster internal and external collaboration and by encouraging people to seek information and opinions beyond their limited department areas, organizations are better equipped to understand the changing needs and expectations of their major stakeholders.

• The people closest to a problem have different insights about the cause(s) of the problem than do those who are at the top of the organization. Therefore, by developing processes that encourage shared decision-making with those closest to the problem, there is a greater likelihood that more effective solutions and decisions will result.

• An organization is not seen as a quality organization unless it has established a culture that encourages assessment and adaptation to the changing expectations of stakeholders. Having in place the seven previous quality principles will go a long way toward establishing a climate of trust. However, without creating processes that foster continuous improvement, this climate of trust will not become a culture for change. As depicted in Figure 7.2, systematic change occurs when the relationships of an approach to an issue, the actions taken, and the results are examined together in context to the vision and mission of the institution. The results of this analysis usually produce evidence or support for some form of change or adaptation. This in turn produces a modification in the approach, and the process cycle continues once again.

By using the principles of a quality culture and the process of continuous adaptation as a contextual focus of the qualitative and quantitative measurements of various institutional processes, institutional leaders can quickly identify specific areas that need to be improved (Chmielewski, Casey, and McLaughlin, 2001). As these principles become an integral part of an organization's culture, the outcomes of the institution will be more closely linked to its vision and mission.

The Values of a Quality Process. An organization's culture is the sum of the values of the individuals within the organization. The principles of a quality culture form a basic framework to reinforce specific values. This section focuses on the values that have been articulated by two quality processes: the Academic Quality Improvement Project (AQIP) of The Higher Learning Commission of the North Central Association and the education criteria of the Malcolm Baldrige National Quality Award. These values are listed in Table 7.1.

Figure 7.2. Cycle of Meeting Stakeholders' Changing Expectations

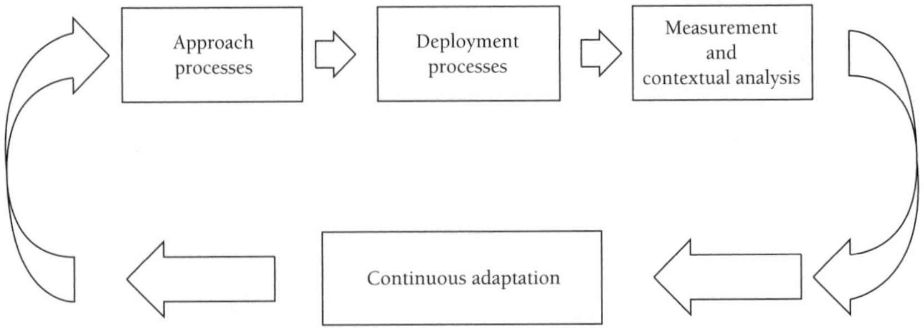

Table 7.1. Principles of a Quality Culture

Academic Quality Improvement Project	Malcolm Baldrige National Quality Award—Education Criteria
Focus—Shared vision and mission.	
Involvement—Ongoing development of people's skills in making decisions, working with diverse groups, resolving conflicts, and using quality-based tools to build consensus.	
Leadership—Top-down/bottom-up.	*Visionary leadership*—Senior leaders should set directions and create a student-focused, learning-oriented climate; clear and visible values; and high expectations.
Learning—Developing everyone's potential talents; centering attention on learning.	*Learning-centered education*—Develop the fullest potential of all students by placing the focus of education on learning and the real needs of students.
People—Prizes and supports the systematic development of its individual faculty, staff, and administrators.	*Organizational and personal learning*—Learning is embedded in the way an organization operates by being (1) part of the daily work life, (2) practiced at personal, work/unit department and organization levels, (3) used in solving problems at their source (root cause), (4) focused on sharing knowledge throughout the organization, and (5) driven by opportunities to effect significant changes to do better.
	Valuing faculty, staff, and partners—Commitment to the development of their knowledge, skills, innovative creativity, motivation, and well-being
Collaboration—Active collaboration among and within different internal departments and operational areas, and externally between the institution and other institutions or organizations.	
Agility—The flexibility to respond quickly to opportunities, threats, and changing needs and practices.	*Agility*—A fast and flexible capacity to respond to the needs of students and other stakeholders.
	Managing for innovation—Making part of the culture and an integral part of the daily work the effort to make meaningful change to improve an institution's programs, services, and processes to create new value for the stakeholders.
Foresight—Tracking trends to better predict how conditions will change; anticipating how these changes may affect the institution's students and other stakeholders, operations, and performance.	*Focus on the future*—An understanding of the short- and long-term factors that affect the institution and its education market.
Information—Seek and use [quantitative] data and [qualitative] information to assess current capacities and measure performance realistically.	*Management by fact*—Decisions are based on measurement and analysis of performance that are derived from the institution's needs and strategy and include critical data and information about key processes and results.
Integrity—Mindful that education serves society, the institution continuously examines its practices to make certain its effects and results actively contribute to the common good.	*Public Responsibility and Citizenship*—An institution has the responsibility to stress ethical practices and protection of public health, safety, and the environment.
	Focus on results and creating value—An institution's performance measurements need to focus on key results that add value to students and other stakeholders.
	Systems perspective—Managing the whole organization, as well as its components, to achieve success by careful alignment of vision and mission, values, and processes.

Source: Academic Quality, 2000; Baldrige, 2001.

The values articulated by AQIP are based on a quality system that is designed to be integrated into the culture and daily practices of higher education institutions. The long-term objective is that through the inculcation of these values into an organization's culture, the traditional regional accreditation process that occurs once every ten years will no longer be necessary. The Baldrige values are based on a quality system that is part of an evaluation or assessment process that creates indicators of the degree to which an institution has successfully developed a systematic approach to quality as part of its culture. Both are values based, and both depend on the continuous use of qualitative and quantitative measurements to put in context an institution's values, vision, mission, processes, and outcomes.

These values operate within the larger context of a system of quality that is comprised of subsystems called *criteria*. The ability to develop contextual qualitative and quantitative measurements is greatly enhanced when these criteria and the interrelationships are taken into consideration.

Quality Criteria Framework. The Criteria Frameworks or Systems of both AQIP and Baldrige are the product of many understandings of what contributes to helping a higher education institution practice on a daily basis what it says it is. In other words, it helps all within the institution live more consciously so that they are more able to achieve their own career goals, which collectively results in achieving the mission of the institution.

AQIP's quality design combines nine criteria that function to produce a quality system. Through the relationship of an institution-wide understanding of student and other stakeholder needs and through the processes of valuing people, leading and communicating, supporting institutional operations, planning continuous improvements, and building collaborative relationships, institutions will help students learn and accomplish other distinctive objectives. However, to function properly, these relationships are dependent on continuously measuring the effectiveness of the institution. Two representations of the interrelationships of these nine criteria are presented in Figures 7.3 and 7.4.

Figure 7.3. AQIP Quality Criteria Framework

| Understanding students' and other stakeholders' needs | Valuing people
Leading and communicating
Supporting institutional operations
Planning continuous improvement
Building collaborative relationships | Helping students learn

Accomplishing other distinctive objectives |

| Measuring effectiveness |

Source: Academic Quality, 2000.

Figure 7.4. AQIP Quality Process and Criteria

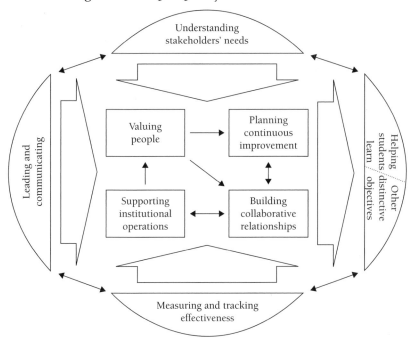

Figure 7.3 depicts the AQIP quality criteria in a linear design, and Figure 7.4 uses a closed-system design. Both designs show understanding students' and other stakeholders' needs at the beginning (or top) of the quality system and measuring effectiveness at the foundation (or bottom) of the system.

The Baldrige education criteria for performance excellence framework is an assessment of an institution's efforts to develop a systematic approach for continuous improvement. As an assessment process, it uses different criteria than AQIP in conceptualizing its quality system. In Figure 7.5 the Malcolm Baldrige National Quality Award framework is depicted.

System Measurements

Both the AQIP and Baldrige models demonstrate the critical role that contextual data and information have to maintaining the dynamic processes of a system of quality. There is a need for quantitative and qualitative information from the beginning (vision and mission), throughout the various process steps, and to the final outcomes. Without information that is presented in the context of what is intended and how things are done, it is unlikely that any meaningful changes can be made to alter the outcomes.

Figure 7.5. Baldrige Education Criteria for Performance Excellence Framework: A System Perspective

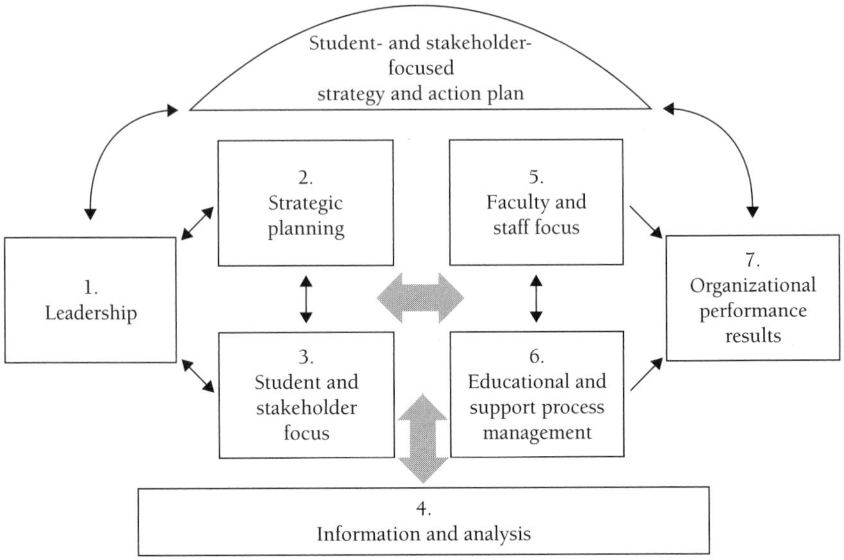

Source: Baldrige, 2000, p. 6.

Contextual information consists of several components:

1. *Baseline data:* These are the data that assess where an organization is at any given time. They are used to develop a context for the impact of activities that occur after the baseline data are collected.

2. *Process measurement:* Gathering these data entails looking at what happens and how it is happening. This information, usually presented in qualitative form, develops a picture of why the results are as they are.

3. *Contextual outcomes or result trend data:* If this information is to be used to alter events in the future, it must be presented in the context of both baseline and process information over a period of time, usually three or more years. When presented this way, trend data have more meaning.

4. *Comparison data:* Institutional outcome data, even if developed in a contextual format with inputs and process information, may not produce successful adjustments to changing stakeholders' expectations and needs if there is no understanding of the processes and results of competing institutions. Therefore, the gathering of external data is crucial to improving internal processes. What types of comparison data should be used will be determined by the end objectives of gathering the comparison data. There are four types of comparison data:

Peer group data is gathered when the objective is to know only how other similar institutions are performing.

Market basket data look at institutions that attract the type of students or research funds that an institution believes it should also be attracting.

Aspirational data are input-process-outcomes data gathered from colleges and universities that an institution aspires to resemble.

Benchmark measurement data are best-in-class data that do not pertain to a certain organizational type but relate to outcome objectives in context with the vision and mission of the institution. For example, if an institution wished to improve the results of teaching a certain scientific principle, instead of looking at another higher education institution, it might look at the training process of a for-profit company that is highly recognized for putting this principle into practice.

Summary

Data and information can be static, measuring a point in time, with no meaning to the dynamics of the organization. If this is the case, these data are subject to being seen as unimportant and therefore ignored or are subject to gross distortions and used for self-serving purposes. Qualitative and quantitative measurements that are developed within the context of the values and vision, mission, processes, and outcomes of an institution result in information that relates to the internal dynamics of the institution. This form of information has meaning, is the basic ingredient for informed decision making, and has a powerful impact on what an institution will become.

For institutions of higher education that are developing a culture of quality, contextual quantitative and qualitative data and information are indispensable. The quality of an institution is determined by how well it meets its major stakeholders' needs and expectations. Because these needs and expectations are constantly changing, there must be a measurement system in place that provides a rational direction to the continuous adaptation needed to meet stakeholders' changing demands. Rational adaptation across the institution is more certain to take place when the appropriate balance of contextual qualitative information and quantitative data-based information guides the development of strategies for adaptation.

References

Academic Quality Improvement Project. Chicago: Commission on Institutions of Higher Education, North Central Association of Colleges and Schools, 2000. [http://www.aqip.org].

Baldrige National Quality Program. *Education Criteria for Performance Excellence.* Gaithersburg, Md.: National Institute of Standards and Technology, 2001. [http://www.asq.org].

Chmielewski, T. L., Casey, J. C., and McLaughlin, G. D. "Strategic Management of Academic Activities: Program Portfolios." Paper presented at the 2001 Association for Institutional Research Annual Forum, Long Beach, Calif., June 2001.

Crowder, M. V., and Janosik, S. M. "Performance Funding in Virginia Higher Education." *Virginia Issues & Answers,* 2001, 7(2).

Deming, W. E. *Out of the Crisis.* Cambridge, Mass.: Center for Advanced Engineering Studies, Massachusetts Institute of Technology, 1982.

Fife, J. D., and Cotter, M. "The Infusion of a Systematic Approach to Quality in Education: Both a Values and Process Approach." Paper presented at the 55th American Quality Congress, Charlotte, N.C., May 2001.

Freed, J., Klugman, M. R., and Fife, J. D. *A Culture for Academic Excellence: Implementing the Quality Principles in Higher Education*. ASHE/ERIC Higher Education Report, vol. 25, no. 1. Washington, D.C.: The George Washington University Graduate School of Education and Human Development.

JONATHAN D. FIFE *has served as an evaluator, senior evaluator, senior examiner, and alumnae examiner for the Malcolm Baldrige National Quality Award Program. He also was a member of the Design Team of the North Central Association Commission on Institutions of Higher Education's Academic Quality Improvement Project.*

8

Reducing uncertainty in decision making is the value added to the management process by institutional research. Effective decision support includes a balance of quantitative and qualitative information interpreted within the decision maker's context.

Integrating Qualitative and Quantitative Information for Effective Institutional Research

Richard D. Howard, Kenneth W. Borland Jr.

Although most of the work done in an institutional research office deals with numeric data, effective decision support requires qualitative information that puts numeric information into the context of the decision to be made. In this chapter we briefly recall the main points of the preceding chapters, which provide a framework for our conclusions and suggestions for balancing qualitative and quantitative information in the creation of effective decision support.

In Borland's comparison of the qualitative and quantitative paradigms, it is clear that once one gets past the philosophical underpinnings of the paradigms, the practical difference between them is not grounded in methodology or in the form of the data (narrative or numeric) but in the generalizability of the results. The purpose of research using the qualitative paradigm is to describe a specific entity or purposely selected persons within a specific context to gain insights about the phenomenon under investigation. In this case, there is no ability to generalize the results of the findings to any other situation or entities by the researcher. If one agrees with Saupe's notion that "the subject of institutional research is the individual college, university, or system" (1981, p. 1), institutional research is thus a form of qualitative research. Further, any generalization of the results of institutional research, either within or outside the institution, is the responsibility of the consumer, not the researcher. Now, it is true that because of similarities of context, the institutional research professional can become the consumer of the research and as such may generalize the results to future events or other programs at his or her institution. However, institutional research paradigmatically is a form of qualitative or naturalistic inquiry.

Illustrating these notions, McLaughlin, McLaughlin, and Muffo describe a program review in which multiple data sources were accessed to evaluate the effectiveness of the program. Their application of the "qualitative *and* quantitative" philosophy when addressing complex questions such as those relating to program effectiveness demonstrates the use of balanced qualitative and quantitative approaches that integrate a variety of data collection and analysis methodologies. The decision support resulting from this balanced approach to evaluating the program is based on multiple data points that reflect not only isolated statistical outcomes of the program but also their relationship to other related findings. In the end, the multiple data points provide a context for the interpretation of any single data point. Further, these multiple data points provide a more complete picture of the program and its relationship to the entire campus, providing information to support decision making at different levels, for example, operational, managerial, or strategic.

In Chapter Three, Howard discusses the environment for creating, formatting, and communicating effective decision support. Specifically, he provides a series of conceptual models that provide different contexts for creating, formatting, and communicating decision support information. Although a number of models are presented, the overriding notion is that to provide quality decision support, an institutional researcher must have a mental understanding of how organizational and decision-making processes are supposed to work. Without this understanding, resulting decision support information will not reflect the organization's or decision maker's structure, processes, or values.

Moss, Ferren and Aylesworth, and Perkins discuss the communication of decision support information from the perspective of the decision support provider and the decision maker. Together these authors illustrate the importance of communicating quantitative information within a qualitative context. A key to meeting this challenge is the need for the institutional researcher and the decision maker to be positioned, both physically and mentally, to communicate both formally and informally on a regular basis.

Finally, Fife discusses the creation of a quality culture in terms of qualitative and quantitative measures that reflect the institution's success in meeting stakeholders' needs and expectations. In this discussion, Fife indicates that qualitative and quantitative trend information about the relationships among inputs, processes, and outcomes allows an organization to identify changing needs of stakeholders.

These chapters produce the following conclusions and recommendations about the role of qualitative and quantitative information in the creation of effective decision support.

Balancing Paradigms and Approaches

A dichotomous paradigmatic perspective is not constructive if the institutional researcher is to provide the most effective decision support. The best institutional research, as outlined in the preceding chapters, is a product of systematic scientific inquiry—a balance of qualitative and quantitative research paradigms and the purposeful use of their approaches and methodologies.

Institutional research is an applied function that in one form or another exists in every postsecondary institution in the United States. In those cases, where the function's responsibilities include the creation and distribution of decision support data and information, the use of analytic tools from many disciplines is commonplace. Although many institutional research professionals have academic training that results initially in the use of familiar methodologies, survival soon requires the acquisition and use of methods from economics, statistics, sociology, anthropology, psychology, management, and any other discipline that will result in providing the most useful information. Acquiring and utilizing the concepts, strategies, and skills associated with both qualitative and quantitative research is another requisite of survival in terms of providing decision makers with the most meaningful and useful information. The institutional researcher cannot afford to sustain a qualitative-versus-quantitative mentality. Instead, his or her attitude toward institutional research should be balanced—qualitative *and* quantitative.

Context and Proximity

Moss, Ferren and Aylesworth, and Perkins suggest that the development of contextual (qualitative) information to support quantitative information is necessary for the decision-making process. The institutional researcher's development of contextual information requires frequent communication with and proximity to the decision maker. This will result in the institutional researcher's understanding of the organization's structure and processes and the decision maker's values. Figure 8.1 is an attempt to illustrate the relationship of qualitative and quantitative research, the organizational proximity of institutional researchers, and the effectiveness of decision support.

The Least Effective Decision Support
The small circle in the lower left of the figure represents an answer to the question "What did you find?" The circle is numeric data or a number representing a relationship between two or more data points. This information from the institutional researcher's analysis has not been placed into a particular context.

To provide this noncontextualized answer to the question "What did you find?" requires the institutional researcher only to utilize what Terenzini (1993) refers to as technical intelligence. Further, the institutional researcher who is asked to provide only a lower level of noncontextualized information (the facts only) need not be organizationally proximal to the decision maker. If data are not expected to be contextualized, the institutional researcher does not need to know the organizational or decision maker's contexts. Data not couched in a qualitative context coming from

Figure 8.1. Creating Effective Decision Support: A Function of Data, Context, and Proximity to the Decision Maker

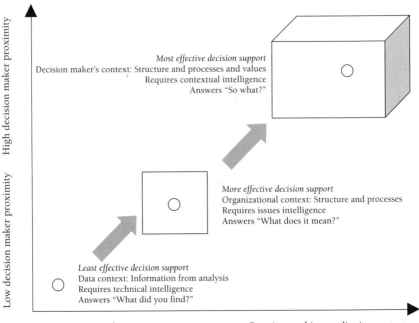

institutional researchers who have low proximity to the decision maker are the least effective form of decision support.

More Effective Decision Support

In the middle of the figure, the same small circle is placed within a two-dimensional box. The circle is still data, but the two-dimensional box represents the organization's structure and processes and context. The data are now contextualized and provide an answer to the question, what does it mean?

To provide this more effective level of decision support, the institutional researcher is required to utilize what Terenzini refers to as issues intelligence. It is qualitative research that enables the institutional researcher to understand the organizational context, the structures and processes into which the numeric data or a number representing a relationship between two or more data points are placed. To place data in the organizational context, the institutional researcher must periodically communicate with and have some organizational proximity to the decision maker. Information and data couched in this two-dimensional qualitative context coming from institutional researchers who periodically communicate with and are proximal to the decision maker foster better decision support than that created at the previous level.

Most Effective Decision Support

In the upper right of the figure, the same small circle is now positioned in a three-dimensional box. Organizational structures and processes as well as the decision maker's values now contextualize the data: this is the decision maker's context. This positioning of the data provides an answer to the question, so what?

To provide this most effective level of decision support, the institutional researcher is required to utilize what Terenzini (1993) refers to as contextual intelligence. Requiring even more qualitative research, the institutional researcher places data in the decision maker's as well as the organization's context. Not only must the structure and processes of the organization be understood, but the values held by the decision maker must also be known. To determine this, the institutional researcher must, organizationally speaking, be located near the decision maker. He or she must have frequent, regular, and direct communication with the decision maker and other senior-level administrators. Data and information couched in this three-dimensional, rich and thick, qualitative context are the most effective decision support.

Enhancing the Environment for Effective Decision Support

Responsibility for the creation of effective decision support is an activity that involves proactive communication on the part of the decision support provider and the user or decision maker. Moss, Ferren and Aylesworth, and Perkins describe active and direct working relationships between the institutional research professionals and the decision makers. The following are some ways in which the two sides of the decision support process can support each other.

For the Institutional Researcher

• *Provide information rather than data.* Data or facts in and of themselves are valueless. It is when they are interpreted within the framework of the decision maker's context that they provide useful information.

• *Present reports in consistent formats.* Most institutional research offices produce periodic reports such as fact books, enrollment reports, and graduation profiles. Periodic reports should also be created and available to campus managers and senior decision makers on a schedule that is consistent with decision-making calendars.

• *Train users to access and use the data.* This will become increasingly important as institutions make data available through data marts and warehouses. To be an effective trainer, the institutional researcher must understand the context in which the data will be analyzed.

• *Discuss with institutional leaders and other decision makers what information is needed, when it is needed, and the most effective way of providing it.*

• *Spend time outside the office talking to managers and leaders.* To understand the context in which decisions are made, the institutional researcher needs to frequently communicate with decision makers across the campus. Understanding both the data and the context in which decisions are to be made will result in the most effective decision support.

• *Develop an ability to communicate at the level of the administrator's interest.* As Moss indicates, important support often is conveyed in impromptu meetings. Unexpected meetings require that the institutional researcher quickly align his or her thinking with concerns of the decision makers.

• Provide mechanisms for evaluating the usefulness of decision support information.

For the Decision Maker

• *Identify needs for information and be available to the institutional researcher.* Whenever appropriate, convey the values, processes, and structures that contextualize the needed information.

• *Communicate values and concerns in relation to the mission of the institution and welcome the decision support person's requests for meaningful contextual details.*

• *Provide feedback about the value or usefulness of the decision support information received.*

• *Provide guidance about appropriate measures to evaluate the impact or correctness of the decision and assess the effectiveness of its implementation.*

Conclusion

Higher education is a complex environment in which multiple stakeholders have different decision support needs. Quality decision support meets these various information needs in ways that are both credible and reliable. Research and analysis is a pragmatic function that seeks to provide information that reduces uncertainty in the decision-making process. This is the value that is added by the institutional researcher. To do this, the institutional researcher must not only describe what has happened or is happening (typically from quantitative analyses) but also interpret these findings within the context of the institution's processes, the organization's structures, and the decision maker's values (from the analysis of qualitative data and information). Maximizing the effectiveness of decision support requires a balance of qualitative and quantitative approaches by the institutional researcher as well as frequent interaction with key decision makers.

References

Saupe, J. L. *The Functions of Institutional Research.* Tallahassee, Fla.: Association for Institutional Research, 1981.
Terenzini, P. T. "On the Nature of Institutional Research and the Knowledge and Skills It Requires." *The Journal of Research in Higher Education,* 1993, *34*(1), 1–10.

RICHARD D. HOWARD is associate professor of adult and higher education at Montana State University–Bozeman.

At the time of writing KENNETH W. BORLAND JR. was assistant vice provost for academic affairs and assistant professor of adult and higher education at Montana State University–Bozeman. Currently he is associate provost at East Stroudsburg University.

INDEX

Back Issue/Subscription Order Form

Copy or detach and send to:

Jossey-Bass, A Wiley Company, 989 Market Street, San Francisco CA 94103-1741

Call or fax tollfree: Phone 888-378-2537 6AM-5PM PST; Fax 800-605-2665

Back issues: Please send me the following issues at $27 each

(Important: please include series initials and issue number, such as IR111)

1. IR _____

_____

_____

$ _____ Total for single issues

$ _____ SHIPPING CHARGES: SURFACE

	Domestic	Canadian
First Item	$5.00	$6.50
Each Add'l Item	$3.00	$3.00

For next-day and second-day delivery rates, call the number listed above.

Subscriptions Please ❑ start ❑ renew my subscription to *New Directions for Institutional Research* at the following rate:

	Individual	Institutional
U.S.	❑ Individual $65	❑ Institutional $125
Canada	❑ Individual $65	❑ Institutional $165
All Others	❑ Individual $89	❑ Institutional $199

$ _____ Total single issues and subscriptions (Add appropriate sales tax for your state for single issue orders. No sales tax for U.S. subscriptions. Canadian residents, add GST for subscriptions and single issues.)

❑ Payment enclosed (U.S. check or money order only)

❑ VISA, MC, AmEx, Discover Card # _____ Exp. date_____

Signature _____ Day phone _____

❑ Bill me (U.S. institutional orders only. Purchase order required)

Purchase order #_____

Name _____

Address _____

_____

Phone_____ E-mail _____

For more information about Jossey-Bass, visit our Web site at: www.josseybass.com

PROMOTION CODE = ND1

IR106   Analyzing Costs in Higher Education: What Institutional Researchers
        Need to Know
        Michael F. Middaugh
        Presents both the conceptual and practical information that will give
        researchers solid grounding in selecting the best approach to cost analysis.
        Offers an overview of cost studies covering basic issues and beyond, from a
        review of definitions of expenditure categories and rules of financial
        reporting to a discussion of a recent congressionally mandated study of
        higher education costs.
        ISBN: 0-7879-5437-3

IR105   What Contributes to Job Satisfaction Among Faculty and Staff
        Linda Serra Hagedorn
        Argues that positive outcomes for the entire campus can only be achieved
        within an environment that considers the satisfaction of all of those
        employed in the academy. Examines various jobs within the campus
        community—including classified staff and student affairs administrators as
        well as faculty—and suggests factors that will promote job satisfaction.
        ISBN: 0-7879-5438-1

IR104   What Is Institutional Research All About? A Critical and Comprehensive
        Assessment of the Profession
        J. Fredericks Volkwein
        Chapters explore the role IR plays in improving an institution's ability to
        learn, review organizational behavior theories that shed light on the
        researcher's relationship with the institution, and discuss the three tiers of
        organizational intelligence that make up IR—technical/analytical,
        contextual, and issues intelligence.
        ISBN: 0-7879-1406-1

IR103   How Technology Is Changing Institutional Research
        Liz Sanders
        Illustrates how to streamline office functions through the use of new
        technologies, assesses the impact of distance learning on faculty workload
        and student learning, and responds to the new opportunities and problems
        posed by expanding information access.
        ISBN: 0-7879-5240-0

IR102   Information Technology in Higher Education: Assessing Its Impact and
        Planning for the Future
        Richard N. Katz, Julia A. Rudy
        Provides campus leaders, institutional researchers, and information
        technologists much-needed guidance for determining how IT investments
        should be made, measured, and assessed. Offers practical, effective models
        for integrating IT planning into institutional planning and goals, assessing
        the impact of IT investments on teaching, learning, and administrative
        operations, and promoting efficient information management practices.
        ISBN: 0-7879-1409-6

IR101   A New Era of Alumni Research: Improving Institutional Performance and
        Better Serving Alumni
        Joseph Pettit, Larry L. Litten
        Drawing from information generated by mail and telephone surveys, focus
        groups, and institutional data analysis, the authors examine various facets of
        an institution's relationship with alumni—including fundraising from
        alumni, services for alumni, and occupational and other outcomes of college.
        ISBN: 0-7879-1407-X

IR100   Using Teams in Higher Education: Cultural Foundations for Productive
         Change
         Susan H. Frost
         Using research and practice from higher education, where teams are used
         with varying degrees of effectiveness, and from business, where teams are
         linked to survival, this issue addresses questions of culture, especially as they
         can affect significant aspects of teamwork. Explores the theory and practice
         related to different types of teams and the dynamics that influence success.
         ISBN: 0-7879-1415-0

IR99   Quality Assurance in Higher Education: An International Perspective
         Gerald H. Gaither
         Presents some of the best quality assurance policies, practices, and
         procedures found in five progressive countries. It offers an international set
         of resources—including Web sites and other electronic resources—to assist
         practitioners in achieving the goals of their own quality assurance
         frameworks.
         ISBN: 0-7879-4740-7

IR98   Campus Climate: Understanding the Critical Components of Today's
         Colleges and Universities
         Karen W. Bauer
         Provides guidelines for effective assessment of today's diverse campus
         populations, highlighting key diversity issues that affect women; racial and
         ethnic minorities; and lesbian, gay, bisexual, transgender, and disabled
         students.
         ISBN: 0-78791416-9

IR97   Performance Funding for Public Higher Education: Fad or Trend?
         Joseph C. Burke, Andreea M. Serban
         Examines the conflicts and issues raised by performance funding as well as
         the similarities and differences in state programs. Discusses the information
         gathered and lessons learned from a national study of performance funding
         supported by The Pew Charitable Trusts.
         ISBN: 0-7879-1417-7

IR96   Preventing Lawsuits: The Role of Institutional Research
         Larry G. Jones
         Examines what institutions and institutional researchers might do to keep
         themselves out of court, although contributors also suggest how institutional
         research pertains when institutions do end up in court. Discusses how
         preventive law—the efforts of attorneys and clients to minimize legal risks—
         may be the most appropriate construct for meeting the needs of institutions.
         ISBN: 0-7879-9876-1

IR95   Researching Student Aid: Creating an Action Agenda
         Richard A. Voorhees
         Provides researchers with the tools they need to make sense of the complex
         interplay of politics, students, and institutions that constitutes our current
         system of student aid. Reports of three empirical studies within this issue
         provide concrete examples of the types of research institutional researchers
         can execute on behalf of their campuses.
         ISBN: 0-7879-9875-3

IR94   Mobilizing for Transformation: How Campuses Are Preparing for the
         Knowledge Age
         Donald M. Norris, James L. Morrison

Provides practical insight and guidance to campus leaders who are attempting to accelerate the transformation of their campuses to meet the challenges and opportunities of the Knowledge Age. This insight is drawn from case studies and vignettes from nearly twenty campuses that have succeeded in leveraging the forces of transformation on their campuses. ISBN: 0-7879-9851-6

IR93 **Forecasting and Managing Enrollment and Revenue: An Overview of Current Trends, Issues, and Methods**
Daniel T. Layzell
Examines demographic, economic, and financial trends affecting enrollment and revenue management and forecasting in higher education, practical examples and issues in enrollment and revenue management and forecasting (for both public and private institutions), current methods and techniques of enrollment and revenue forecasting in higher education, and an evaluation of lessons learned in these areas.
ISBN: 0-7879-9850-8

IR92 **Assessing Graduate and Professional Education: Current Realities, Future Prospects**
Jennifer Grant Haworth
Despite its burgeoning popularity, the assessment movement has focused largely on undergraduate education, leaving institutional researchers, administrators, and faculty with scant information on methods for conducting assessments of graduate and professional education and a dearth of the results of such assessments.
ISBN: 0-7879-9899-0

IR91 **Campus Fact Books: Keeping Pace with New Institutional Needs and Challenges**
Larry G. Jones
Explores ways in which the campus fact book can remain and grow as a significant institutional research report, both in light of new reporting demands and opportunities and in response to new and increased demands and uses for institutional data and information from and by internal and external constituencies.
ISBN: 0-7879-9900-8

IR90 **Faculty Teaching and Research: Is There a Conflict?**
John M. Braxton
Examines empirical evidence concerning the relationship between faculty research activity and such facets of their teaching as classroom performance, teaching preparations, the influence of teaching behaviors on student learning, faculty goals for undergraduate education, faculty attitudes and behaviors concerning their interactions with students, pedagogical practices, course assessment activities, norms delineating inappropriate teaching behaviors, and adherence to good teaching practices.
ISBN: 0-7879-9898-2

IR89 **Inter-Institutional Data Exchange: When to Do It, What to Look For, and How to Make It Work**
James F. Trainer
Highlights the benefits and risks associated with participating in inter-institutional data exchanges and describes the various types of exchanges that are available.
ISBN: 0-7879-9874-5

IR88   Evaluating and Responding to College Guidebooks and Rankings
R. Dan Walleri, Marsha K. Moss
Explores issues surrounding college guidebooks and ratings. The
background and development of these publications are traced, followed by
discussion of major issues and perspectives—consumer use of the
publications, validity of ratings, and the institutional burden of supplying
the needed information
ISBN: 0-7879-9944-X

IR87   Student Tracking: New Techniques, New Demands
Peter T. Ewell
Describes important changes in the requirements for student tracking data
bases and examines the expanding technical possibilities provided by
statewide administrative data bases and by the availability of greatly
enhanced data-manipulation and statistical tools for constructing and
analyzing longitudinal data files.
ISBN: 0-7879-9943-1

IR86   Using Academic Program Review
Robert J. Barak, Lisa A. Mets
Provides planners and institutional researchers with information on the uses
of program review results in colleges and universities.
ISBN: 0-7879-9920-2

IR85   Preparing for the Information Needs of the Twenty-First Century
Timothy R. Sanford
Offers reference points for the institutional researcher and planner as
postsecondary education plunges into the twenty-first century. Charts possible
ways the world of higher education may evolve in the next ten to fifteen years.
ISBN: 0-7879-9919-9

IR84   Providing Useful Information for Deans and Department Chairs
Mary K. Kinnick
Argues that institutional researchers need to give more attention to deans
and department chairs and suggests methods for providing them with the
information that will help them to understand changing student needs;
facilitate and assess student learning; assess and understand faculty culture;
and redefine, assign, and assess faculty work.
ISBN: 0-7879-9989-X

IR83   Analyzing Faculty Workload
Jon F. Wergin
Explores how the public discourse about faculty work might be improved
and suggests how colleges and universities might document that work in a
fashion that not only more faithfully describes what faculty do but also
allows for reports that are more comprehensive and useful.
ISBN: 0-7879-9988-1

IR82   Using Performance Indicators to Guide Strategic Decision Making
Victor M. H. Borden, Trudy W. Banta
The goal of this issue is threefold: to provide the reader with an
understanding of what has led to the current popularity of indicator systems;
to illustrate several possible methods for developing performance indicators;
and to synthesize theory and practice into a formulation for a proactive,
institution-based approach to indicator development.
ISBN: 0-7879-9964-4

IR78   Pursuit of Quality in Higher Education: Case Studies in Total Quality
        Management
        Deborah J. Teeter, G. Gregory Lozier
        Provides valuable insights into the experiences of colleges and universities
        that are applying the principles of Total Quality Management (TQM) to
        higher education. Presents different aspects of TQM regarding issues of
        organization, training, use of tools or methodologies, the language of TQM,
        or the challenges in transforming organizational cultures.
        ISBN: 1-55542-693-X

IR66   Organizing Effective Institutional Research Offices
        Jennifer B. Presley
        Designed to assist both those who are establishing an institutional research
        function for the first time and those who are invigorating an existing unit.
        Provides major guidelines for how to approach tasks and avoid major
        pitfalls.
        ISBN: 1-55542-829-0

IR61   Planning and Managing Higher Education Facilities
        Harvey H. Kaiser
        Provides information on facilities management for institutional researchers,
        with theories and application covering a range of topics from a global
        perspective to specific issues.
        ISBN: 1-55542-868-1

IR55   Managing Information in Higher Education
        E. Michael Staman
        Describes many of the key elements in the development of an information
        management program and the policies and procedures that must be in place
        if the program is to be successful and sustainable over time.
        ISBN: 1-55542-947-5